LIVING
IN THE STATE OF
STUCK

*How Technologies
Affect the Lives of
People with Disabilities*

MARCIA J. SCHERER

BROOKLINE BOOKS

Library of Congress Cataloging-in-Publication Data

Joslyn-Scherer, Marcia S.
    Living in the state of stuck: how assistive technologies affect the lives of people with disabilites / by Marcia J. Scherer
      p. 189 cm.
    Includes bibliographical references and index.
    ISBN 0-914797-84-0
    1. Physically handicapped -- Rehabilitation -- United States.
2. Self-help devices for the disabled -- United States.
3. Technological innovations -- United States. I. Title.
HV3023.A3J67 1993
362.4'0483 -- dc20

                             92-41986
                              CIP

Published by
Brookline Books
P.O. Box 1046, Cambridge, MA 02238-1046

Table of Contents

Section I:
Physical Aspects of
Spinal Cord Injuries and Cerebral Palsy

Section II:
Assimilating Persons with
Disabilities into Mainstream America

Section III:
Future Directions

**"There ain't nothin' worse than being stuck.
There's nothin' you can do to change it physically
and you know that right off the bat.
And when you ain't got nothin' to fight with,
then you loose your will."**

Butch, a 38-year-old male paralyzed by a spinal cord injury, speaking four years after his injury from an automobile accident

Acknowledgments

I owe much and obvious gratitude to the individuals who participated in my research project. Because I am only a conduit for their experiences, ideas and recommendations, it would be unfitting for me to profit from the publication of their material. Therefore, all royalties from the sale of this book are being donated as follows:

50% to the National Spinal Cord Injury Association and
50% to the United Cerebral Palsy Associations

In addition to the participants in this study, I thank the following:

The National Science Foundation for sponsoring the original study upon which this book is based,

Faculty at the University of Rochester and the National Technical Institute for the Deaf for their helpful guidance (especially Drs. Thomas Knapp (now at Ohio State) and Barbara McKee. Thanks are extended to Drs. Ruth Weissberger, Harry Lang, William Welsh and Susan Foster who provided very useful feedback on earlier drafts of this manuscript.

Dr. Milton Budoff, Publisher and Editor, Brookline Books, for this patience and invaluable guidance — and for publishing a line of books which share the purpose of advocating for persons with disabilities.

And, finally, my deepest appreciation — as well as affection — to John Scherer, who truly started it all.

The material in this book is based upon work supported by the National Science Foundation under grant RII-8512418 sponsored by the Ethics and Values in Science and Technology, and Biotechnology and Research to Aid the Handicapped programs.

Foreword

Marcia Scherer persuasively reminds us that as technology is used to increase opportunities for individuals with disabilities to become productive members of society, the needs of the whole person must be taken into account. For assistive technology to provide the maximum benefit, services that address the emotional, personal, and social needs of the individual in adjusting to and using these devices must also be provided.

SENATOR TOM HARKINS
Chair, Subcommittee on Disability Policy
Committee on Labor and Human Resources

Preface

by Frank Bowe

Fifteen years ago, when I was the chief executive of the American Coalition of Citizens with Disabilities (ACCD), then a major Washington, DC-based umbrella lobby group, I hired a bright young woman to run our rehabilitation training programs. The best I could do to accommodate her cerebral palsy was to provide her with a keyguard to fit over her electric typewriter. A few years later, Rita Varela took a job with GTE in Florida. By that time, personal computers had become commonplace in the office. The PC — with its quick-and-easy error correction, spell-checker and function keys — liberated Rita. For the first time in her life, she was able to produce work that reflected her intelligence and knowledge. Rita quickly became an expert in computer programming. She even wrote a book in her spare time explaining how to use a PC to perform advanced mathematical functions. *Victory Over Statistics* (GTE, 1989) is impressive enough a work. What makes the book even more meaningful to me is what it represents—the fact that with technology, Rita achieved victory over cerebral palsy.

This idea—that an individual with a disability, plus the right device, can function as a person without limitations—had fascinated me for some time. It compelled me to write *Personal Computers and Special Needs* (Sybex Computer Books, 1984), the first full-length text on high technology and people with disabilities. The book's theme still strikes me. I see it in action when friends of mine who are blind or severely learning disabled listen to the synthesized speech produced by their PCs, rather than trying to read the screen. I see it when other friends with quadriplegia talk to their PCs, rather than type. And I hope soon to see it when I and others who are deaf read on a screen what others say.

When—as is now happening—technology removes limitations, what we as individuals with disabilities can do depends strictly upon our abilities, training and experience. The devices liberate us to become what we optimally can be. At the same time, these products render vacuous any excuses we might have used before. We are forced to confront the fact that our lives will be what we make of them. We become responsible for ourselves. When we exercise that responsibility in work, in our families, and in our communities, we achieve the real meaning of independent living.

This relationship between technology and people with disabilities raises a lot of difficult questions. Marcia Scherer explores many of these issues by showing what people with disabilities do with technology — and what technology in turn does to them.

Among the questions that are emerging now is that of who should pay for the new devices. The fact that someone like Rita Varela can use a PC to perform gainful employment suggests that it is in society's best interest to provide her with the devices she needs. With them, she is no burden to the taxpayer; indeed, until she died a few years ago, she paid her fair share of payroll and other taxes, helping to support others in our society.

As a subset to that question, should we link government payment for technology to an individual's commitment to, in effect, pay us back by working? That is, should no-cost technology be available only at the workplace and, by extension, at schools and job-training programs? If we answer that question affirmatively, we are limiting the "right to technology" by circumscribing it to conditions under which society realizes a return on investment.

There are arguments on all sides of these questions. One could say, for example, that someone like Rita should purchase the special aids she needs from her take-home pay. Alternatively, one could say that someone who needs technology uses it not only to work but also to live a more meaningful and rewarding life. Indeed, people with very severe disabilities may not even be employable. Tying technology to work denies such individuals any access to no-cost devices. Society should provide these people, under this argument, with technology they need regardless of whether or not they work.

To illustrate, the Television Decoder Circuitry Act of 1990 [P.L. 100-431] requires that all 13" or larger television sets sold or manufactured in the United States after July 1993 include built-in chips enabling the set to receive and display captions or subtitles. The chips themselves cost under $10 to manufacture, and are included as part of the purchase price of the set. Broadcasters, advertisers and others pay the cost of producing the captions themselves. Our nation made a national policy statement in that Act: T.V.s are an important enough part of American society today that we should make it accessible to all of us.

Should we take the next step and make television equally as accessible to blind and low-vision individuals? The Education of the Handicapped Act Amendments of 1990, P.L. 101-375, authorized demonstrations of what is called "descriptive video service", in which one audio channel of a stereo T.V. is used to broadcast spoken descriptions of the video action blind people cannot see. Descriptive video service remains experimental. Should we do with D.V.s what we did with captioning?

But personal devices are only part of the story. More and more, we are finding that we can use the telecommunications infrastructure to provide important accommodations for people with disabilities. By equipping telephone company central offices and switching stations with speech synthesis, speech recognition, and other important capabilities, we can make those functions available to virtually all Americans with communication-related disabilities — at very little or even no added cost to them.

To illustrate, Title IV of the Americans with Disabilities Act of 1990 [P.L. 100-336] requires that all 1,600 telephone companies in America ensure that deaf people and others using telecommunications devices for deaf people (TDDs) have full and equal access to all telephone-based services. By July 1993, TDD users must be able to make and receive calls to and from all 50 states, 24 hours a day, 7 days a week. Title IV provides TDD users with these services at no incremental cost to them.

Suppose we said that access to remote bulletin boards (RBBs), electronic databases, White and Yellow Pages and other information over telephone lines must also be equally available, at no extra cost, to blind and dyslexic individuals who cannot read E-mail and other messages on a screen? That individuals with severe cerebral palsy or other disabilities that limit or prevent intelligible speech have the right to this same network-based speech synthesis, in this case, to "talk" for them? If we agree that these are appropriate national policies, we will need to amend the 1934 Communications Act to carry them out. The ADA's Title IV did its work by adding a new section 225 to that Act.

These are some of the questions that will help to shape the debate on reauthorization of the Technology Related Assistance for Individuals with Disabilities Act of 1988, P.L. 100-407. TRAIDA was America's first-ever legislation specifically about technology and people with disabilities. It authorizes modest sums of money for the states to use in educating people with disabilities about products, and in putting technology experts in touch with individuals who need those devices. States receiving TRAIDA money must obey Section 508 of the Rehabilitation Act, as amended in 1986 and again in 1992. Section 508 requires that any office equipment or information services purchased, leased, rented or otherwise acquired by federal agencies and by units of government in states receiving TRAIDA monies must be accessible to and usable by individuals with disabilities.

If we decide to expand our national commitment to making technology more readily available to all Americans with disabilities, we will have to go well beyond the current policy as expressed in TRAIDA and in Section 508. Are we prepared to do that? For example, we could say that not only television sets but any electronic product or computer-based service sold or made in the United States must be accessible to individuals with disabilities. We have already said that about buses, train cars, and most buildings. In the so-called Information Age, should we treat electronic products any differently than we now do public transit vehicles and aspects of the built environment?

Marcia Scherer's contribution in this volume is to illuminate these issues for us, by showing how they emerge in the real lives of individual human beings. As tantalizing as many of the emerging technologies are, we cannot just hand them to people with disabilities, any more than we can introduce Coke bottles into a culture that has no organized disposal system. The introduction of high technology into the lives of individuals with disabilities often has unexpected and indeed unforeseeable consequences. That is why Dr. Scherer emphasizes that technology alone seldom is the answer.

Still, we are asking guestions that never occurred to me when I was trying to accommodate Rita Varela's typing limitations. Maria Scherer's gift to us in this book is that she stimulates us to ask good questions. As always, the hard part is not to answer but to ask the right questions.

Frank G. Bowe, Ph.D., is professor, Department of Counseling, Research, Special Education and Rehabilitation, Hofstra University. His most recent book is *Equal Riqhts for Americans with Disabilities* (Watts, 1992).

Introduction

by Peter Axelson

If you are involved, or want to be involved, in the prescription, fitting, modification, or design of assistive technology, you will learn something from this book. If you are new to the field, you will gain information on spinal cord injury, cerebral palsy, and a brief history of the rehabilitative process, including the independent living movement. If you have been involved in design without dealing with the personalities of thc clients, you will learn about how people with disabilities feel about assistive technology, and how their attitudes affect their acceptance of the technology.

Funded by a grant from the National Science Foundation, Marcia Scherer studied assistive devices from the perspective of the people who use them. Meeting, interviewing, and participating in the lives of people with different functional limitations, Scherer observed how these people used technology to enhance their functions in their daily activities. As Scherer relates people's stories, you will learn how the attitudes, experiences and circumstances of individuals affect the daily choices they must make about personal, assistive, or adaptive equipment for work, school, recreation, and everyday life.

People whose function is significantly limited (so that viable alternatives do not exist) have the highest rate of assistive technology usage. For others, psychological factors, including everything from their background to their acceptance of their loss of function, will affect the choices they make on personal assistive and adaptive equipment.

The author theorizes that individuals must acknowledge their loss of function before they are willing to seek out, use, or design assistive devices. People may reject an assistive device because it identifies them as having a disability. To be effective, Scherer emphasizes, assistive technology must not only foster independence and autonomy but also contribute to a positive identity and enhanced self esteem.

Assistive technology experts are truly in a unique position to improve and change the lives of the people they work with. With these clients, they can serve as facilitators, enabling clients to use assistive devices to make their lives work better. "People with disabilities have found assistive technology to be important enablers in achieving a high quality of life."

Scherer suggests these ways to improve users' attitudes toward assistive technology:

- Give users more information about the advantages and disadvantages of specific technologies.

- Give people a trial period to use a new device in the environment — home, work, outdoors — where they will use the device in their lives.

- Schedule follow-up visits to help consumers refine and tune a device for their specific needs.

- Put new users in touch with peers who use similar technology.

- When training new users of technology, end each training session with a positive experience.

"There has been an explosion of the number and types of assistive technology and an expansion of their flexibility," Scherer notes. She suggests that users should have a greater role in the design and prototyping of technology if it is to be more functional and better accepted by those it is intended to serve. Above all, her book emphasizes, the technology, however helpful it may be in its design, cannot function without acceptance from potential users.

Peter Axelson, Ph.D., is Director of Research & Development, Beneficial Designs, Santa Cruz, CA.

Author's Introduction

A change came over the spirit of my dream.

Byron

For many individuals with disabilities, life itself depends on a pacemaker, a respirator, or a kidney dialysis machine. For others, technology has enabled them to speak for the first time in their lives, to walk again after paralyzing accidents, to read books any time they want and to communicate with anyone in the world even though they are without sight or hearing. Technology has helped people with physical disabilities more than they ever thought possible — not just to survive severe exposures to illness and trauma, but to function physically as if they had no limitation in function.

Technology was meant to free people— to allow people to extend their abilities, to manage their lives more effectively. It raised the hopes of many for a better and easier life. This is especially true for those with physical disabilities. But the physical freedom offered by many technical products and advances has not resulted in the higher quality of life technologists envisioned. This book shows how, paradoxically, the more technology became available and the more free from physical limitations individuals with disabilities became, the more stuck many seemed in several important ways.

This book shows what the lives of people with disabilities are REALLY like — their thoughts, fears, goals — in their own words. It does not provide a general overview of the current issues in rehabilitation or disability studies. It takes one issue, the burgeoning growth in technologically based forms of assistance, assistive devices. It discusses how technology is experienced by the people who use them. Technology has revolutionized the lives of people with disabilities. What professionals, users of this technology, and their families should do to introduce and support the use of this technology to improve the **quality of life** of those with disabilities is the purpose of this book.

The major message is that machines and assistive devices provide important assistance to persons with disabilities, but individuals must be prepared for technology use. People with disabilities may benefit from counseling to understand their current situation and the contribution technologies offer. They require ongoing consultation so the proper use of the devices can be monitored and adjusted as the needs of users change. This counseling and consultation place the user at the **center** of the process of assistive device provision.

TECHNOLOGY IS THE ANSWER, BUT THAT'S NOT THE QUESTION

It was 1977, the year I received my master's degree in rehabilitation counseling, and my husband, an electrical engineer and a physically Disabled American Veteran, was reading an article in a trade journal about computerized devices to help people with disabilities. "Here's an article I'd like you to read. I think this is going to be a big thing in the future," he said.

He certainly was right! I read that article, and all the others he passed on to me. (Interestingly, it would be several years before articles on such assistive devices would appear in my rehabilitation journals). As time went on, I became increasingly concerned that issues of quality of life — individuals' emotional, personal and social needs — were being neglected in favor of technical solutions to the needs consumers presented to their rehabilitation agencies. I made the decision to try and find out more.

It was for the purpose of pursuing my concern that the National Science Foundation awarded me a research grant to study the perspectives people with disabilities have about assistive devices, current definitions of "rehabilitation success," their "disabled experiences," and their quality of life. Since this was a study designed to discover rather than assume the important factors involved, I worked with a small group of people with disabilities. At the time of my initial study in 1986, all were adults between the ages of 21 and 45, half of whom were born with their disability (cerebral palsy); the remainder incurred their disability in adulthood (spinal cord injury). In addition to interviewing, testing, and observing these persons, I also spoke with their rehabilitation engineers and primary therapists over the course of the next six years to learn how their lives were changing.

Brief description of the study[1]

Participants were observed in their rehabilitation centers, homes, or work sites to understand how they perform with or without the use of assistive technologies in their daily activities. Observation and interview notes were kept on whether or not they use assistive technologies, on the ease, comfort and effectiveness of use, and on the conditions and circumstances under which they experience difficulties. At the time of observation, in-depth interviews were also conducted according to a pre-defined interview schedule.

ASSESSMENT OF PERSONAL CAPACITIES. Each participant was asked to complete the Personal Capacities Questionnaire (PCQ) (Crewe & Athelstan, 1984), a 30-item measure surveying six functional areas: Adaptive behavior, vocational qualifications, communication, motor functioning, physical condition, and cognitive functioning. Two additional items assess visual impairment and the need for special job requirements. Respondents were asked to read a list of ten personal strengths and to check all they believed applied to them. Finally, respondents rated their perception of the severity of their disability and their "chances of getting and holding a job" on two Likert scales (7- and 4-point respectively).

ASSESSMENT OF TEMPERAMENT. Participants were also asked to complete the Taylor-Johnson Temperament Analysis (T-JTA) (1966-1985), a 180-item inventory that profiles the respondent on nine traits (and their opposites): Nervous/composed, depressive/light-hearted, active-social/quiet, expressive-responsive/inhibited, sympathetic/indifferent, subjective/objective, dominant/submissive, hostile/tolerant, and self-disciplined/impulsive.

Data from the instruments and interviews were used to produce comprehensive descriptions of individual perspectives and characteristics. Patterns of individual results were then compared to assess commonalities or differences in assistive technology use, personal capacities, temperament and perceived quality of life.

The individuals who participated in the study are truly transition people. For the most part they grew up during the pre-mainstreaming years and before people with disabilities were extended civil rights.

Many of them are pioneers in the use of assistive devices and worked actively with their therapists — and continue to do so — to fabricate their own equipment.

While this book portrays only a short time span of six years, it is special because it describes these issues as they are being encountered during this transitional period. Many issues and problems recounted in this book didn't exist before the 80's; most may either be resolved or non-existent in the next century. For now, they define the lives of almost all people with physical disabilities.

Initially, I tried to approach this study as a detached researcher. However, as the individuals in this book slowly grew to trust me and began to share increasingly intimate details of their lives — their thoughts, feelings, and fears — I found myself caring and feeling and noticed that I, too, was changing.

AN OUTLINE OF THE BOOK

This book chronicles the changing lives of these persons; a continuing process. By the time these accounts are read, these people will have changed again. They may have entirely new perspectives and experiences.

In *Chapter One*, the lives of Chuck and Brian, two men with spinal cord injuries from motorcycle accidents, are contrasted. They are both classified as "quadriplegic," but they do not have identical injuries and limitations and they use different assistive devices. As a result, they also have had different experiences and available opportunities.

Chuck and Brian had once lived without disabilities. They were seriously injured as adults. Thus, many things they do now, by comparison, take longer and require more effort. As they strive to compensate for their losses, they continually confront limitations in themselves and limitations in assistive devices.

Jim and Maggie, on the other hand, were born with cerebral palsy and have always had their disabilities. They tend to focus on gains and newly found capabilities. In *Chapter Two*, they describe their experiences with devices, and how they view some of the new options available to them today.

In *Chapter Three* the history of the care and rehabilitation given to individuals in the United States is traced. While governmental policies and societal attitudes have over time pendulated in their humanitarianism, we are currently at a point, due in part to assistive devices, when people with disabilities are becoming more visible throughout society. Visibility is one thing; assimilation, however, is quite another.

In *Chapter Four*, differing perspectives of rehabilitation success are presented. Definitions of "rehabilitation success" need to be changed: not just society's, but those used by rehabilitation professionals and by people with disabilities themselves.

Chapter Five discusses the concept of *quality of life* and illustrates the concept with examples from the lives of several individuals with disabilities. While their issues and concerns are individualized, they share concerns around independence and interdependence.

Many frustrations and challenges experienced by people with disabilities may be the same as those of non-disabled individuals, yet they differ both quantitatively and qualitatively. The problems of persons with disabilities are usually more frequent, more difficult to deal with, and often have more severe consequences. Their issues and concerns may mirror those of non-disabled persons, but the issues are frequently magnified.

Chapter Six discusses the ways in which people learn to adjust to or cope with their disabilities. Individuals respond in ways that reflect learned patterns for need satisfaction, their personality characteristics and the expectations others have of them. Some may experience cycles of hope; others despair. These influence one's view of opportunities, growth, and the use of technological and other assistance. Taken as a whole, they eventually characterize a person's quality of life.

In *Chapter Seven*, the reasons people with disabilities give for using or not using assistive devices are discussed in terms of the **Matching Persons and Technology (MPT)** model. This model provides a framework for comprehensively assessing the characteristics of the m*ilieu* or environment, *person*, and *technology* which influence an individual's use or non-use of a particular assistive technology.

The last chapter, *Chapter Eight*, summarizes issues and concerns expressed by these people with disabilities and discusses their ideas for changing the focus of rehabilitation efforts to more broad quality of life considerations. Changes are needed in order for all of us to emerge from this time of transition with an enhanced quality of life.

Throughout this book I present the experiences, ideas and hopes of people with disabilities, their therapists and engineers, in their own words, so as not to speak for them, but to help give their voices a forum. This points out the need to address current preferences in terminology used when discussing individuals with disabilities. While such phrasing as "persons with disabilities," "coping," and the "disabled experience" have their proponents and opponents, I have tried to select words that are not "stigmatizing" and put *persons* first, yet are familiar to most readers.

Finally, though the names and other identifying features of the persons quoted throughout this book have been changed to protect their privacy, their statements and experiences have not been altered in any way. The goal of this book is not to persuade or convince but to stimulate thinking, discussion, and perhaps even argument. To argue, after all, is to become involved; to become involved is perhaps to care.

REFERENCE NOTE

[1]   Detailed information on the "participatory action research (PAR)" design (Graves, 1991; Whyte, 1991) used in this study and the research procedures, instrumentation, and data analyses can be found in the articles listed in the *References*.

Section I:
Physical Aspects of Spinal Cord Injuries and Cerebal Palsy

CHAPTER ONE

Going Into the 21ˢᵗ Century with a Disability

What man that sees the ever-whirling wheel
Of Change, the which all mortal things doth sway,
But that thereby doth find, and plainly feel,
How Mutability in them doth play
Her cruel sports, to many men's decay?
Edmund Spenser

Imagine that you are suddenly unable to perform your usual activities, to go out to dinner with friends, to laugh and talk over something that happened at work, to cut your own steak and feed yourself. Then imagine having *never* done these things, even though you're 20 years old.

This is reality today for millions of Americans. And tomorrow it will be reality for more — perhaps someone very close to you.

This book shows, through the experiences of many persons who "tell it like it is," what life is like today for individuals with severe physical disabilities. For example, twenty-nine year old Chuck was having an average day until, in the span of just a few hours, he left a rather carefree life of riding his motorcycle, tending bar, and gadding about with friends for one where he will never again be able to walk, feed himself, even go to the bathroom alone. Chuck's story, in his own words, tells what he believes it is like to go into the 21st century in a way very different from anything he had ever imagined — in a way in which he is totally unable to control and move on his own every single muscle between the tops of his shoulders and the tips of his toes.

CHUCK, 1986

Before... okay, I was only tending bar. But to me, I was a success. I was happy with my life at the time. I didn't plan on being a bartender forever, but for then it was just the right thing I needed to get away from the stress of business. And I was having a good time. Probably the best time of my life.

I'd been separated from my wife for a year-and-a-half. Late one night I was riding my motorcycle and the next thing I knew I was in the hospital. I never knew what happened, and no one else was ever able to figure it out. My best guess is that some guy ran me off the road and I crashed.

I was aware of being sandwiched between two slices of board and being turned every couple of hours. My spleen and one kidney were gone. I could speak and hear and see, but that was about it. The thing was, I didn't even know what was going on. I was still confused about myself and my condition and I had everyone coming in and saying, "We're going to educate you to do this, help you to do that." I didn't even know what I wanted to do, could do, at that point.

For someone like me, paralyzed from the shoulders down, therapy should have been more practical — like taking us out to a grocery store or something like that where there are people around. And I wish I'd had counseling regularly... on a fairly regular basis. I'm not sure what would've come out of it, but if you see someone enough, eventually you're going to say something — try to bring things out, some of the anger, and things like that. That was something that was never done, and that anger just sits in there and grows.

Oh, they did have a psychologist on the floor. I think his name was Lloyd. I saw him once, and the major reason for that was because I smoke and didn't want to quit. He came in and said, "Well, maybe we should mark down whenever you have a cigarette." For Christ's sake. Didn't he see that I couldn't smoke without someone on the floor giving me one and holding it in my mouth for me?

From the moment of that accident on, I was no longer an independent person. It's like... I have a typewriter, to use an example. Okay, now I know that everyday I should spend some time putting the mouthstick in and just keep pounding on it — even if it's just 25 minutes — to keep the endurance in my neck up. But I don't always do that. Twenty-five minutes just goes somewhere else. I'll say, "I think I'll go have an extra cup of coffee." Other times I'll get involved and work for two hours straight. It's no different from when I was out in the business world working. I mean there were things I probably should've done and I'd say, "I think I'll go have an extra cup of coffee," or "I'll do it tomorrow." And everybody does the same thing. But when you're in this condition, people say to you you've got to do it NOW. They don't look at it like they're looking at themselves, and saying, "I can put it off until later." No, it's "let's do it now" with "you have to do this, you have to maintain that." Screw it! I'll do it when I get to it. I wasn't that organized before, so why should it change now? I know what has to be done and when it has to be done and that's what I work on. Your basic style doesn't change just because you're in a wheelchair and the only things you can move are from the neck up.

I was in a state of shock all through rehab and, truthfully, I'm still in a state of shock. Sometimes I sit here and ask, "Why did I ever live through this?" I think I'm depressed a little bit more... more than 50% of the time. To get myself out of it, I make myself do something to get away from the four walls that are closing in. So, there's the TV again. Do you know what I mean? Before the accident, I never watched that much TV and after it's like, "there it is again."

I've talked with lots of quads, about my level, and everyone seems to agree they would rather have not been saved than to be in the situation they're in now... to be so dependent. And there are a lot of times I feel the same way.

I try to make the best of what I've got, but on the other hand, I look at my friends that I used to play football with, or baseball, or something, and they're still doing it. I go out to lunch with them now and get treated like a helpless kid or something. And that makes me feel even worse. Because then I wish that I could stand up, just for a couple of minutes, so I could tell them to shove off.

But when you're in this condition, you have to accept their ideas of help to a certain extent so your friends don't feel too guilty. You have to let them accept it on their own level. At least that's my experience, with my friends.

On the romantic side, women have a tendency to move away from me... It's like, "see ya' later." I mean, it's easy to find someone to say, "okay, let's go out," but when it comes to the romantic side of it, they're not sure what to do or what to expect. Too, it's hard to approach somebody when you're in a wheelchair, as opposed to the way it was before. I mean, what do you say? Can I buy you a drink, and by the way, would you help me with mine?

Even my one-year-old niece. She doesn't understand the wheelchair and so she's kinda leery of it. And I just wish she'd come up and grab me and give me a hug.

I find now that I identify with disabled people a little bit more than I did before. Even after my open heart surgery and car accident, I was always the type of person, if I saw someone in a wheelchair, I was probably like anyone else and it was like, "Hi, how're you doing." I wasn't really careful with what I was saying. I did know a couple of guys in wheelchairs and I look at them a lot different now than before. Then, I'd kid around a little and things like that and now it's more like I really know what they're talking about when they say things.

I seem to notice people a lot more, too. Even someone on crutches sticks out more to me now than in the past. It's not like I look over their heads anymore and just cruise on by. Now I search their faces... and look more in their eyes.

PEOPLE WITH DISABILITIES: OUR LARGEST SUBPOPULATION

Chuck is just one of approximately 35 million Americans (one in every seven) with a disability severe enough to interfere with life's day-to-day activities (Institute of Medicine, 1991). And each year the numbers go up. For example, the incidence of severe disability increased more than 70% from 1966 to 1979, from 213 individuals per 10,000 population to 365 (Fenderson, 1984).

Relatively recent advances in medical science, trauma care, and technology have allowed lives to be saved, maintained, and extended as has never before been possible. Adults who were born with disabilities are living well into middle-age and older. Hazards of modern living (automobile accidents, airline disasters, and other traumas) cause severe injuries that people are surviving, but with permanent disabilities. And, as increasing numbers of people live longer, we see more disabilities associated with advanced age.

The chances of persons spending at least a portion of their lives with a disability are greater every day. For example, The University of Michigan's Transportation Research Institute has reported that during a typical 75-year life span a person is sure to be involved in a traffic accident (every 19 seconds, someone in the U.S. is injured in an automobile accident). The same individual has a 1-in-50 chance of not surviving this accident, and a whopping 50-50 chance that he or she will suffer a disabling injury. Injuries received in motor vehicle accidents are the leading cause of death for more than the first half of the life span (ages 1-44). Injury treatment and rehabilitation is also the most costly of all major health problems in the U.S.

When risk ratios for other traumatic and disease exposures are studied, it appears that many of us will be functioning with a severe disability or limitation in function at some point in our lives. We are two to four times more likely to have a permanent disability (one lasting longer than 90 days and, on the average, over 6 years in duration) than to die before the age of 65. There is a 60% probability of having a permanent disability between ages 30 and 65.

Americans with disabilities are currently our largest minority group. The population of disabled Americans had grown close to 35 million according to the Census Bureau's 1985 statistics. In that same year there were approximately 29 million African-American persons and 17 million Hispanic people in the United States. While there were 365 individuals with severe disabilities of all types for every 10,000 non-disabled Americans in 1979, or 36,500 per million, in 1986 there were approximately 30-35 persons with spinal cord injuries alone per million non-disabled Americans. Quadriplegics (like Chuck, who is paralyzed from the shoulders down) comprise half of these individuals living with spinal cord injuries.

PHYSICAL ASPECTS OF SPINAL CORD INJURIES

There are now approximately 200,000 people in the U.S. with spinal cord injuries and between 10,000 and 20,000 new incidents reported each year (Institute of Medicine, 1991). Experiences in the treatment of battlefield casualties during World War II and the Vietnam War have directly led to an increased rate of survival for all people with spinal cord injuries. Survival has been enhanced by important developments in emergency medical care and very early intervention by emergency medical personnel, specialized trauma centers and multidisciplinary rehabilitation centers. Advances in the control of infections and other conditions secondary to a traumatic spinal cord injury have served to increase the likelihood that persons with severe spinal cord injuries can live well into middle-age and beyond.

As Chuck said when talking about his hospital stay, ". . . everyone [was] coming in and saying, 'We're going to educate you to do this, help you to do that.'" In a comprehensive rehabilitation unit, available in many major hospitals across the U.S., each spinal cord injured patient has an entire team of professionals working to help preserve and enhance as much sensation and as many motor and other functional abilities as possible. This team can consist of physicians specializing in emergency, internal, neurological, orthopedic, urological, and rehabilitation medicine (or physiatry) and can also include nurses, physical therapists, occupational therapists, social workers, psychologists, and vocational rehabilitation counselors. If the individual is fortunate enough to be in a Regional Spinal Cord Injury Center (there are fewer than 20 in the U.S.), the individual has this team from the very beginning. The usual course would be: stabilization of the person's medical condition and the treatment of associated injuries; then the person is taught and shown ways to be independent in spite of what may be many functional physical limitations; finally, the team guides the individual through discharge planning and assists in planning for the provision of follow-up care once the person is back in the community.

The causes of spinal cord injuries are many, but basically fall into two broad categories: *pathological*, due to disease processes, and *traumatic*, due to injury. Such pathologies as transverse myelitis, infection (abscess), and tumors can permanently damage the spinal cord, which is the main pathway for the nerves to the neck, arms, diaphragm, thorax, abdomen, pelvis, and legs. Traumatic spinal cord injuries originate from automobile and motorcycle accidents, sports injuries, gunshot wounds, and falls. The Regional Spinal Cord Injury Centers differ in the proportions of individuals they see in these two categories as well as in the origins of pathological and traumatic conditions. In the category of traumatic spinal cord injuries, the Detroit Center, for example, primarily saw injuries from gunshot wounds in 1984 whereas in Rochester, NY there were mostly injuries from automobile accidents; on the West Coast, sports injuries predominated (Scherer, 1984).

Due to the primary causes of traumatic spinal cord injuries, men are involved at a rate four times that of women. The mean age at injury is about 29 years, with half being injured before the age of 25.

The course of each spinal cord injury is unique. Not only do few similar injuries result in the same losses of motor function and sensation, but individuals react and adjust to their injuries in a variety of ways and over varying lengths of time (Krause & Crewe, 1987; Trieschmann, 1988). There are several factors that serve to define and classify types of spinal cord injuries anatomically and functionally to guide treatment planning. One factor, the "motor neurological level", indicates both the location of the injury along the spinal cord and the lowest muscle with normal function. For the purpose of this classification by functional level, the spinal cord has been sectioned into four zones that, from top to bottom, are a) cervical, b) thoracic, c) lumbar, and d) sacral.

As shown in Figure 1, there are many segments within each zone. For example, the cervical (C) zone has eight segments that serve the neck,

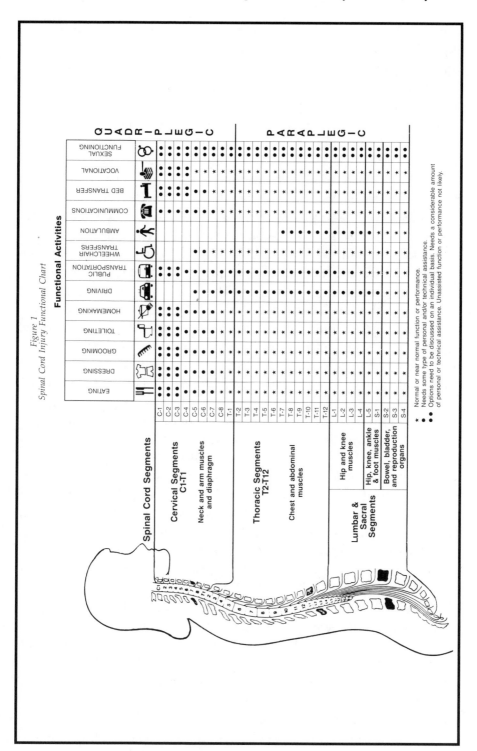

Figure 1
Spinal Cord Injury Functional Chart

arm and diaphragm. The highest injury within the cervical zone (and along the entire spinal cord, since the cervical zone is the highest zone) is in the upper neck area and is classified C1; the lowest (in the upper back area) is C8. The C7 vertebra can be felt easily at the base of the neck as it protrudes further than any other.

It is still quite rare to have survivors of complete injuries at and above the C3 and C4 segments. An individual with preserved function at the C4 level, such as Chuck, is essentially paralyzed from the shoulders down with little or no sensation or motor function any place below the level of the injury. Persons with injuries at the C5 and C6 levels fare better (Kottke, Stillwell, & Lehmann, 1982). They can be expected to get themselves in and out of their wheelchairs with some personal or mechanical assistance and can drive a car with special handcontrols and other adaptive equipment. Individuals with preserved function at the C6 level can perform some grasping activities. Those with a C7 or C8 classification can work with their hands independently and may have functioning triceps (the upper, outer arm muscles we feel when doing push-ups) to get themselves in and out of their wheelchairs independently. The presence or absence of functional triceps is a critical determinant for functional independence in self-care tasks (Welch, Lobley, O'Sullivan & Freed, 1987).

Cervical spinal cord injuries result in a condition known as *quadriplegia*, which means all four quadrants of the body (two arms, two legs) have muscular paralysis. *Paraplegia*, on the other hand, refers to paralysis in the body's two lower quadrants — the person has little voluntary movement below the waist and has paralysis in both legs. Spinal cord injuries at the mid-thoracic level or below frequently result in paraplegia. The lower the functional level of the injury, the more voluntary motor control and muscle power is available to the individual.

Hemiplegia is a term that also indicates two-quadrant paralysis, but on one side of the body. Right-sided hemiplegia means a person has paralysis of the right side including the right arm and leg. Hemiplegia is not an outcome of a spinal cord injury; it is the result of an injury to that side of the brain opposite the side of weakness or paralysis — i.e.right-sided paralysis indicates the brain was injured in the left hemisphere. Strokes, tumors, birth injuries (such as cerebral palsy) and other traumatic injuries to the brain may cause damage that can lead to hemiplegia or, if more severe, to quadriplegia.

The suffix *paresis* instead of *plegia*, as in *quadriparesis, paraparesis* and *hemiparesis,* indicates that the individual does have some movement in the involved quadrants and that the paralysis is slight or incomplete. "Incomplete" injuries suggest that some motor and/or sensory functioning below the zone of injury has been preserved and there has been some return of sensation (the ability to receive information from or through the body) — or some controlled motor function — the ability to make one's muscles and body act. A person with an incomplete injury may feel heat and someone's touch and may have numbness or weakness in affected muscles instead of paralysis. If there is preserved sensation only, then the person has some sensation below the level of injury, but complete loss of voluntary motor control. Advances in trauma and medical care have resulted in increasing numbers of *incomplete* rather than *complete* injuries.

Complete injuries indicate that the spinal cord has been so severely cut, bruised or crushed that there has been no preservation of either motor function or sensation below the zone of injury. Involuntary muscle control — the kind that keeps our hearts beating without us having to think about it — is a brain activity and, thus, is not "paralyzed" by a spinal cord injury.

Uncontrolled movements such as simple reflexes can cause a person's legs to move, or jerk, in response to stimulation. It may be nothing more than the touch of bed clothing. This is called *spastic paralysis*. It can make the leg, for example, quiver and jerk uncontrollably for many minutes at a time. Unfortunately, such spasticity is not an indication that motor functioning is returning. Rather than being a positive sign, these spasms or uncontrollable episodes of jerking are more a source of annoyance and embarrassment to individuals who may have such spastic reactions many times a day. For this reason, many individuals with spastic paralysis are given muscle relaxants, such as valium, to minimize the number and duration of spastic episodes.

A Spinal Cord Injury is a Lifelong Health Condition

Even such explicit terms as *quadriplegia* and *C4 Complete* can be applied to a variety of patterns of functioning. One such pattern is represented by Chuck, whose spinal cord is damaged at the C4 level, and who is able to voluntarily move only the muscles of his neck, face, and head. Unlike some C4 injured individuals, Chuck can breathe without the assistance of a respirator. Besides having so little controllable movement, Chuck has no sensation of any type below his level of injury including the abilities to feel pain, temperature changes, and touch. Thus, Chuck can no longer shave or dress himself. He requires help from others — either family members, friends, or hired personal attendants — for all of his toileting and bathing needs. His ability to get around is limited to where his wheelchair can take him.

From Chuck's standpoint, his environment is "a totally controlled one." His privacy is essentially non-existent. When he wants a cigarette, he needs someone to light it, hold it to his lips, and extinguish it. Because of his inability to move at will and to sense, he has no control over his bladder and bowel. A spinal cord injury for Chuck, and all people with severe high level spinal cord injuries, is a lifelong health condition that requires regular and serious attention to prescribed daily programs of diet control, rest, physical exercise, and personal hygiene. Otherwise, such preventable and treatable conditions as pressure sores, respiratory problems, coronary disease , and urinary tract and kidney infections are apt to create serious and recurring medical problems that can lead to frequent hospitalization, a series of periods of interrupted time from work or a training program, and even premature death [Walker & Kokhar, 1992].

The Hospital Often Becomes a Second Home

Chuck and I first met four years after his accident, but he had been in the hospital for several months recovering from a surgical procedure. While we were talking, hospital professionals of many types came in to chat and kid with him and inquire into his physical needs — and, I remember thinking, to be protective of him. Once my tape recorder had been spotted, my ID badge was scrutinized by one of Chuck's young, freshly trained attending physicians who, in a very polite, yet firm professional manner, inquired into my identity and purpose for being in Chuck's room. Clearly, they cared about Chuck's well-being and were guarding against his being made uncomfortable or being exploited in any way.

At one point during another of our conversations, a nurse came in with some medication dispensed with the following plea:

"No more tricks now, okay."

I was curious to know what she was referring to, so I asked Chuck what she had meant.

"You aren't one of those guys that uses the cheek as a pouch and then spits out the pills later, are you?" I was aware, even as I asked the question, that it sounded flip, insensitive.

> No. She was talking about the night I had the Code Blues. I went into cardiac arrest. They think it was a reaction to one of the medications they gave me. But they don't really know for sure what happened. I wish they did.

Chuck's matter-of-fact tone and acceptance of this emergency situation startled me. Perhaps he sensed this.

> Oh, that wasn't the first time that's happened. A couple of other times I've died and been resuscitated.

Chuck, just 33 years old, was certainly no stranger to hospitals — nor apparently to physical distress and even death. When he was 19 years old he had open heart surgery for a blocked aorta. Eight months after his heart surgery he was in an automobile accident and sustained lower back injuries. He was 29 years old when he had the motorcycle accident that resulted in his C4 spinal cord injury and he has been in and out of the hospital since. In addition to his heart problems, he has had his spleen and one kidney removed.

The calm, good-natured man in this room had certainly been through plenty of trials. Can it be surprising, then, that the hospital staff desired to befriend him — and to protect and shield him from any further calamity?

For Many, Assistance Comes in a Variety of Forms

While Chuck requires and depends on others to help him with activities people without disabilities take for granted in doing for themselves, he can achieve some privacy and independence by taking advantage of recent advances in technology. He uses a battery-powered wheelchair, activated and controlled through a joystick extension and operated by his head movements, since he has no controllable movement below his shoulders. When Chuck wants to turn right, he places his head against a crescent-shaped bar that extends from one side of his head, around the back to the other side of his head, and applies pressure to that part of the bar near his right ear. When he gets to an elevator, he grabs his mouth-stick with his teeth, sets it on the elevator button, and with a forward head movement presses the elevator button. Chuck's power wheelchair is an assistive technology. It alone gives Chuck control over much of the mobility lost in his motorcycle accident.

ASSISTIVE TECHNOLOGIES OR DEVICES are mechanical, electrical, or computerized tools for enhancing the routine functioning of people who have physical limitations or disabilities. When people speak of high-tech **assistive devices, assistive technologies,** or **rehabilitation technologies** they are usually referring to those with electronic components. Computers *per se* are not considered assistive technologies. Rather, they are an **access technology**. Many devices operate and work through the control of a computer.

There are several ways to categorize assistive technologies: One is the degree of customization required — from a uniquely fabricated device to modifications of those available "off the shelf." Another depends on the functional purpose for which the device or assistive technology is prescribed. Three examples are:

1. **Mobility devices**: power wheelchair systems, vehicle control systems, sonic guides, vision enhancement devices, and Functional Electrical Stimulation (FES). In FES, successive bursts of low level, controlled, electricity stimulates paralyzed muscles to contract according to patterns programmed into a computer. This allows the return of coordinated movement to paralyzed muscles, such as for walking. It is used with persons whose muscles have not been damaged and with persons, such as those with spinal cord injuries, whose movement has been blocked by the inability of messages from the brain to get through the spinal cord and to the muscles.

2. **Augmentative and alternative communication (AAC) systems**: technologies that enable a person with limited speech or no useable speech to visually display their words or speak through synthesized or other means of speech output.

3. **Sensory devices**: reading devices for people with visual impairments; personal FM systems for persons with hearing loss.

When individuals with disabilities are prevented from acting independently and attaining personal goals due to their own limitations, or to limitations in environmental and social accommodations, such persons are said to be "handicapped." Due to the increased availability of electronic, computerized, high-tech assistive devices, however, government data suggest that even though people with severe disabilities (like Chuck) are becoming more prevalent throughout society, they are becoming less handicapped. Such devices have provided some relatively easy solutions to formerly complicated rehabilitation problems and are very popular with both clients and rehabilitation professionals. Statistics from a nationwide survey revealed:

> In 1969, 6.2 million people used a total of 7.2 million assistive devices. With the advent of the microcomputer in the late 1970s, the number of devices has multiplied" (University of Wisconsin-Stout, 1984).

Each passing year has seen the numbers of assistive technologies in use increase exponentially.

As it became more and more evident that the interest in and need for assistive devices would keep growing, a new field, rehabilitation engineering, was created to design and outfit devices while studying and monitoring their general feasibility. Many Rehabilitation Engineering Centers operate in the United States, each with its own core area of research such as "worksite modification," and "wheelchair systems and specialized seating."

Helping people with physical disabilities go into the 21st century is now as much the domain of science and technology as it is that of medicine and vocational rehabilitation. Without assistive devices made possible by relatively low-cost electronic components and computers, many people with physical disabilities would be leading isolated and dependent lives. For example, today a person with functional movement of the arms and shoulders and above (C6 or lower injuries), can live alone, travel, and work in a competitive job due to advances in technology. As recently as the early 1960's, most equipment available to individuals with disabilities was only of a mechanical nature. Wheelchairs were literally chairs on wheels. Artificial limbs were plastic or, earlier, metal and wooden replacements for lost arms or legs.

Generally speaking, *prosthetic devices*, such as artificial limbs, replace or substitute a part of the body (like arms and legs). *Orthotic devices*, such as braces, are used to provide support for a weak part of the body. *Assistive devices* are just what the term implies — they assist individuals in performing certain functions like getting around in wheelchairs and in specially designed vans. *Adapted equipment* refers to devices designed for the general population which are adapted in ways to be useful for people with disabilities (for example, eating utensils with built-up handles). Some adapted devices are so widely used and accepted we don't think of them as "adapted equipment" at all. For example, an adapted equipment specialist for the United Cerebral Palsy Association in Rochester, NY noted:

> We all use adapted equipment. Take for example the pencil I'm holding. It allows ideas in my brain to be recorded on paper. But millions and millions of people cannot use this pencil; generally they're in the first grade. So what do we do? We make larger pencils for them that they can hold. We give them a piece of adapted equipment. If there's enough people who can't use something, it will be adapted.

The distinctions among these terms are far from pure. Further, whatever distinctions may have existed twenty years ago have likely become blurred with advances in technology. However, electromechanical or computerized assistive technologies generally refer to devices that attempt to compensate for sensory and functional losses by providing the means to move (wheelchairs, lifts), speak (voice synthesizers), read (Opticon systems for people who are blind), hear (vibrotactile aids for deaf persons) and manage self-care tasks (automatic feeders, environmental control systems).

Brian, 1986

Today, a person with a spinal cord injury, especially the individual with voluntary movement in the arms and shoulders (injuries at the C6 level and below), can live and function with considerable independence. One example is Brian, who has an incomplete C6 spinal cord injury from a motorcycle accident he had in 1978 when he was 17 years old.

> It was a sunny, t-shirt and light jacket kind of day. I had finished a busy week moving people out of their apartments and into new ones, cutting people's lawns, painting houses and doing various odd jobs. I was 17, working as a rent-a-kid, and had a fast and busy schedule. The money was good that summer, but being a normal kid, I looked forward to the weekends.

I had a few hours to kill and it was hard to stay inside on such a nice day. Sitting in the garage was a red and black Honda dirt bike which I had shared with my Dad for the last two years. For Dad, it was simply a toy; for me, it was the one vehicle which gave me an adult-like freedom and independence. With a swift, even motion of my right foot on the kick start, I fired up the engine and headed out towards a well-known bike trail.

Gunning the bike, I fishtailed from the trail onto a long disused railroad bed, the tracks having been ripped out ten years earlier. I had an exhilarating sense of well-being as I headed west doing 35 mph in 3rd gear. That was the last thing I remember.

After waking up from a two-week-long coma, the first thing I remember was lying face-down on a Stryker Frame with 35 pounds of traction bolted to my head and being rotated every so often. It was cold and bright. Saliva was dripping out of my mouth into a basin on the floor, and a respirator was attached to my throat pumping air into my lungs. My friends sat on the floor trying to keep me comfortable by just being there. I wasn't able to talk with all the drugs they put me on, plus my vocal cords were paralyzed. I didn't know where I was or what had happened at this point.

The days passed by in a continuous struggle to survive. I suffered three respiratory arrests and at one time my heart stopped for 6 seconds.

I felt helpless in a body that wouldn't move. The doctors said there was little hope I would ever regain anything back. I had lost my memory and was like a child again. My mother would read to me everyday. She read from the book, *The Other Side of the Mountain*, which was a comfort and inspiration to me and to my mother. One day a few of my closest friends brought a cassette tape that included some of the music we always used to listen to, hoping it would engage some recognition of the past. Right before they would leave it would be turned on. All alone I would listen to Marshall Tucker, Flying Burrito Bros., and the Grateful Dead. After listening to the tape several times, small fragments of the past were piecing together.

Each day had its ups and downs and slowly I was regaining my strength but, more importantly, my mind. For a while, I would communicate by use of a wordboard.[1]

Four months had passed and I finally found myself on a rehabilitation floor. By that time my mind was in full flight, but still I was too weak to sit in a wheelchair. The first things I thought about were skiing, taking drives, and going to concerts because those are the things I did with my friends. It wasn't a matter of 'How am I going to put on my pants again?' — things like that were really secondary.

My friends came up to visit as usual and said that [my favorite group] the Grateful Dead were playing here in November. My mind was back, but I had to get my strength. The doctors said I would have to sit 4 to 5 hours straight if I were to go to the concert. My ambition to go was strong and I had to work for it. Every time I got in the wheelchair, I blacked right out. Each day for only a short time I would sit in a semi-reclined position determined to reach my goal. After a couple of days I was up to three hours. The day of the show I reached my goal and I was psyched. The concert was the first time I had been out of the hospital. I had reached my destination.

Thus began my second life. The first was one of standing and being active, and the second life is one of being in a wheelchair. The second life is the one where I realized you can't take life for granted. You have to make each day count to its fullest. That's why I try to accomplish at least a couple of things each day, even if they're small things.

At the time of this interview, Brian was single and living with his parents in his own apartment on one side of the family house. It was constructed especially for him (according to his own specifications) by his father, an architect. There is a private entryway into his two-room apartment (a bath and a bedroom/office), with a ramp leading from his door to the driveway.

There's no other place around here that can match it, and a lot of the apartment buildings aren't accessible to people in chairs. Strangely enough, before my accident, I pictured having a room here. Everything was the same — the wood paneling, deerskin on the wall, stuffed owl and the potbelly stove — except there were mountains in the back.

Looking around, I noticed that Brian's apartment overlooks a large wooded backyard with several bird feeders dangling from the branches of the trees nearest the house. Inside, he has a parakeet, several plants, and a sophisticated stereo system all in a space about the size of a large bedroom. In addition to the deerskin, his walls are covered with colorful posters and the bright colors and variety of textures and shapes made his room look just like a student's dorm room as well as a mountain lodge.

His place was designed to be a serious work and study area, not a retreat, and his desk is crammed with several inches of books and papers strewn along the top. Brian is studying for a degree in manufacturing engineering technology and is, apparently, a good student: His employer for his cooperative work experience told him that Brian could expect a permanent job there upon the completion of his degree program.

Brian, while not what anyone would call a "handsome" man, is what everyone would consider an "attractive" man. He is very thin, almost gaunt. The preppie attire on such a lanky frame, combined with a well-trimmed beard, call forth images of sportsman-cum-student. He has no other medical conditions, and he takes "only typical quad medications like valium for spasticity."

An average day for Brian starts when he pulls himself out of bed and into his power wheelchair with the assistance of an overhead trapeze bar. While he can move only his head, neck, shoulders and arms, he is able to groom and dress himself with the use of such aids as zipper pulls and velcro closures on shirts and pants — and even his shoes, which he can grasp and slide onto his feet with a pistol-grip reacher. Once dressed, Brian goes into the kitchen to prepare and eat his breakfast. He then grabs a jacket and his books and heads out to the garage to his van — a vehicle designed to accommodate both him and his power wheelchair and where he operates everything (acceleration,braking, etc.) by hand controls.

In the way one opens the trunk of a car, Brian inserts a key (with a built-up handle) into a slot towards the rear of the passenger side of the van to activate a switch that slides open the side doors. Another turn of the key lowers a hydraulic lift. Brian removes the key and eases himself into place on the lift and locks his wheelchair in place. He activates a switch to raise himself to the level of the floor of the van, once there activates another switch that automatically closes the door, then wheels into position behind the steering wheel, locks his wheelchair into place, and, through adapted hand controls, starts the ignition and drives off to work. For Brian, this van is a major bridge to independence.

> I can't tell you how much my van has helped me see the light in so many ways. Before, I had the motorcycle — and I drove that everyday. I had that independence, and all of a sudden it got struck down. Here I was stuck. I'm fortunate I had that [power wheelchair] to get me out when I needed to get out. Now that's just expanded with the van. I can come and go whenever I want to.

Once Brian arrives at school or work he is able, thanks to ramps and elevators, to access almost any building, floor, and office he wishes. Once in his own office, a special desk allows his wheelchair to slide under it so that his wheelchair becomes his desk chair as well. On the desk is Brian's computer, which can give him access to anyone in just about any place in the world.

> It's mind boggling when you think of the things that they're coming up with. What higher-level quads like me couldn't do before we can do now. What a big incentive to keep going. There are so many advantages. [He paused, grinned, and added,] I mean, I'm glad I broke my neck in this century.

Brian places a high value on his assistive devices and sees them as keys to his independence. When I told him that some people choose not to use them, he seemed surprised.

> Eventually, what people see as optional devices now are going to be seen as essential. I'm shocked to hear that some people would actually turn something down that's available to upgrade their functioning. And I'm curious why. It totally baffles me.

In spite of Brian's many assistive devices and his independence, he acknowledges that a lot of physical and emotional challenges remain.

> It takes twice as long, three times as long for me to do a simple thing [like getting in his van and driving off to work]. It takes a lot of time and definitely a lot of patience, especially when things aren't going right. There are times when I'll be working at the desk and things will fall on the floor, repeatedly. It's just like, 'screw you.' I just have to laugh at myself because when I do that it makes me feel better and I get control back. I pick up the papers and think, 'Hey, this is a game...' Really, you've got to play it as a game... 'Someone's up there and they're messing with my head...' It's all what you make of it, how you perceive it.
>   You see, if I come across something that needs to be done, or that hinders me in any way, then I find a way that'll work. Rather than using a reacher, sometimes I can pick something up off the floor faster just by bending over and manipulating it just so. But a lot of people can't do that. I was blessed with long arms. It's all a matter of technique.

In the winter, Brian particularly enjoys using his long arms and technique at sit-skiing. This is a sport just like downhill skiing, except Brian is always in a seated position with his legs extended outward in front of him. His seat is a fiberglass sled with ski-like runners. He sits in the sled with poles taped to his hands, and, tethered to an able-bodied assistant, is able to downhill ski. He controls his skiing through the use of his poles and by shifting his body weight. Through this adapted equipment, Brian is able to enjoy — and participate — in a sport we usually associate with strong leg muscles and agile movements.

During his other leisure hours, Brian goes out with friends. However, he feels he's grown away from his old friends and he says he'd like more opportunities to talk with someone about his "private feelings."

> I especially wish I had a girlfriend. It would be all that much... more. It would definitely give me a better perspective. You know, where I could share things with her and she could share things with me. Right now I'm just me, myself, and I know someday it'll happen, it's just a matter of when. It'll happen, just like everything else happens. That's an experience I've learned.
>
> Not too many people have their life planned out for them like I've planned it out for myself. You can't dwell on the past; you can't dwell on the future, but you can't let it go either.
>
> I get depressed. I think, 'I wish I could live a normal life' — but then I realize I do live a normal life. Even better than normal. I think, 'I wish I could lead an active life' — but then I realize I do live an active life. At times I wish I could get out and frolic in the snow — but I do frolic in the snow, because I go skiing.
>
> You have to plan for the future. That's one of the things that makes me want to get up in the morning... having something to shoot for.

TWO DIFFERENT PEOPLE, TWO DIFFERENT FUTURES?

Unlike Brian, Chuck cannot live a fairly independent life. The level of Chuck's spinal cord injury and the fact that, unlike Brian, he has no voluntary control over the movements of his shoulders or arms, means that he needs a lot more assistance than what assistive devices alone can provide. Brian primarily utilizes assistive devices whereas Chuck relies mostly on personal assistants. For example, Chuck requires the assistance of someone — a family member, friend or paid personal assistant — to get him out of bed and into his wheelchair in the morning and to help him get dressed and groomed. He also needs someone to prepare his breakfast. However, with the use of assistive devices, particularly the more high-tech ones, Chuck can ultimately be less dependent on others for many of his activities.

Chuck can have control over when his coffee is ready in the morning by using the same system designed for the general population — a coffeemaker with a timer that can be set the night before. An environmental control system (ECS) can be customized especially for Chuck through the use of different types of switches. Depending on the amount of functioning and gross and fine movement a person has available, environmental control systems can be operated through a mouthstick, a puff-and-sip pneumatic control (for those with enough ventilatory control), or through a voice-activated mechanism. Each ECS has the capability to remotely control a variety of household appliances such as a coffee maker, TV, radio, lights, automatic dialing telephones, and intercoms.

In the morning, Chuck could open the door for his personal assistant by using his ECS to release the front door lock. He could have the coffee ready so that his assistant just needed to pour it into the cup for him. Currently, prototypes of robotic and expert systems are being developed to perform many of the routine functions done for individuals by their assistants.

Chimpanzees and monkeys have been trained to perform some of these same functions. While they have more capabilities than current computerized systems, but less than a personal assistant, they are rare in the homes of persons today.

After Chuck's assistant helps him in grooming and dressing, he can either be fed by his assistant or eat his breakfast independently through the use of an automatic feeding device. Once his food is placed in a special ridged and sectioned plate, a computer-activated device (that works along the same principles as a phonograph record on a turntable) assumes control of the feeding process. The plate is revolved to a certain point or setting where a spoon is attached to an arm slot control. When the plate has stopped in the preselected setting, the arm (just like the tone arm on a record player) moves down to scoop up the food in the spoon, then raises it to mouth level so Chuck can have a portion of food. This isn't a fast process, but it does enable Chuck to enjoy independence in eating. It frees his assistant to work on something else for him.

After breakfast, Chuck requires his assistant's help in cleaning the feeder and the kitchen in general. But once he's groomed, dressed, and fed, Chuck, too, can independently access his own van — using full head, not hand, controls. The differences in cost between Chuck's van and Brian's are great. Chuck's need for such devices as an automatic feeder and an environmental control system make the costs of his independence much higher in general than Brian's. This applies to a work setting, too, because not only would Chuck need a specialized desk to accommodate his wheelchair, but he requires all his work tools to be connected to a computer so that everything can be activated by his mouthstick.

Work stations for higher level quadriplegics like Chuck are very elaborate because users with such limited functional movements cannot access a large working radius. However, items can be set on turntables (like Chuck's plate on his automatic feeder) that can be moved into an accessible position by the push of a computer button. With this done, Chuck's computer, like Brian's, can give him access to anyone, anywhere in the world.

As these examples show, high-tech products have been a boon in enabling individuals with physical disabilities to lead more independent lives. But their individual stories also highlight the fact that not all persons with disabilities can benefit equally from technology, and certainly not with identical amounts of financial resources. Chuck's assistive devices need to be more complex, and thus are much more expensive than Brian's. Too, while Brian can take advantage of newer high-tech devices, in some cases he can choose to use a simple reacher or, as he said earlier, to pick up an object off the floor "just by bending over and manipulating it just so." Chuck does not have as many options and would lead a much more confined and restricted life than he does now if not for his personal assistants and assistive devices.

It is important to keep such distinctions in mind when comparing the opinions people have of their assistive devices. At times Chuck gets irritated with his devices and focuses on their limitations and faults because he can exercise so few choices around their cost, level of technical sophistication and even whether or not he can try to get along without them. And when he does use his devices, his options socially and recreationally cannot come close to those of someone like Brian — who, in spite of his many capabilities, has bouts of depression and shares Chuck's feelings of being restricted, especially in the area of intimate relationships.

REFERENCE NOTES

[1]   A typical wordboard is a stiff, flat surface that contains the letters of the alphabet, numbers 1-10, and perhaps many key phrases such as

'thank you,' 'I want,' and so on. It is small and light enough to hold in one's lap. The user of a wordboard communicates by spelling out words. This means of communication is more fully described in Chapter Two.

CHAPTER TWO

Independent For The First Time

Success is counted sweetest by those who ne'er succeed.
Emily Dickinson

Chuck and Brian are just two examples of young adults going into the 21st century with disabilities. Their lives may seem restricted and incomplete compared to their earlier years. But for some individuals who have had severe disabilities since birth or shortly thereafter, opportunities were rarely available for them to do anything on their own. Jim, born with cerebral palsy, was diagnosed as mentally retarded. His parents were advised to institutionalize him because he would need permanent custodial care. He learned to feed himself at 19 and to drive at 21. At 25 he was hired as an accountant for a major insurance company.

Jim, 1986

Jim, now 34, has severe cerebral palsy (CP) that involves all four quadrants of his body. He is "quadriparetic," meaning he has some control over the movement of his muscles in those quadrants. I knew from talking with him over the phone when arranging our meeting that his speech intelligibility is poor. Like many people with CP, he sounds like a record played at too slow a speed. In addition, his words are ill formed as if spoken with a thick tongue. The speech muscles of many people with CP are weak and difficult to control.

Jim said it would be most convenient for us to meet in his office and that the best time would be from noon to one, during his lunch hour. He expressed a strong conviction that our meeting should not interfere with his work time.

The huge main floor of his building was filled with suited executives hurrying among the live full-size trees, modern sculptures, and escalators. There was a constant din of inaudible conversation buzzing by. Elevator bells were popping at the rate of an automatic weapon, each detonation bringing what sounded to be a corps of the infantry storming towards the yet unopened doors. The place was frenetic.

Jim had given me detailed directions to his office, but I really wasn't sure how to get there because I was too reluctant to ask him to keep repeating the directions. I figured that once I got inside the building I'd either be able to figure it out for myself or find someone to direct me.

I got off the elevator on the fifth floor and felt relief at the contrasting quiet and calm. There wasn't a single person in sight, so I decided to turn right towards a set of closed doors that looked into a large area that appeared to be partitioned into office cubicles.

As soon as I was inside those doors a figure suddenly appeared and said, "Hi. You must be Marcia. I'm Jim's friend, Paul." His hand was waiting to shake mine and his smile was relaxed and warm in spite of his carefully crafted "dispassionate professional" image: three-piece suit, starched white shirt and broad-shouldered, straight-backed young executive posture. He said that Jim's office was just a few steps to our left. I noted it was the first office anyone would come to when entering that wing of Jim's department.

Jim was sitting at his desk waiting for me. An attractive man with long blond hair and classic facial features, he greeted me with friendly charm. He, too, was wearing a three-piece suit, but his ensemble included a bright colored shirt with a pattern. It was obvious that Jim needed a shave, and the muscles in his mouth were weak so that when he spoke he drooled — which would cause Paul to come to his assistance with a tissue.

I recall trying to picture a Type-A business person meeting with Jim. How many people, I wondered, would feel comfortable working with Jim and would have the patience to listen to Jim's slow, slurred speech?

We stayed in Jim's office just long enough for him to show me the adapted equipment he uses to do his work. Other than a few low-tech modifications such as a modified computer keyboard and a telephone with oversize buttons, he went about his job tasks like any other accountant. I recall that his office was sparse in decor, and remember noticing only papers, reports, and computer printouts strewn about. He had a communication device, but told me he doesn't use it because

> Around here, you have to keep up a fast pace. If you call and get a machine, what do you think? You usually hang up. Also, people don't want to take the time.

I didn't tell Jim that I find such augmented speech preferable to not understanding — or misunderstanding — someone. I figured if there were any real problems, his supervisor would have made Jim aware of them by now.

Jim said that we had been given the use of a conference room in the next wing for our meeting. He is ambulatory but walking is a slow and physically strenuous process for him. Therefore, Jim often uses an "electric scooter" to give him speed in getting around the building. His scooter is a powered three-wheel vehicle with a chair and armrests, has handle bars similar to those on a bicycle, and a bicycle-type basket to carry papers, printouts, his briefcase, and other items. For crosstown trips and for getting between his apartment and work, Jim drives his own fully-equipped van.

We went down the corridor and into the next wing. We passed several of his colleagues who either acknowledged us with a smile and a head nod, a greeting, or a joke. Later, Jim asked me,

> At your job, when you walk down the halls, does everyone keep talking to you all the time like that?
>
> I don't know... I guess so, Jim. What do you mean?
>
> Well, a lot of times I'll be trying to concentrate on something, I'll be deep in thought, and they'll interrupt me. Is it just me, or does everyone have that?

Jim wanted reassurance that he was truly being greeted as a colleague and not as a "handicapped person in need of cheery pick-me-ups all the time."

Once we were in the next wing, a secretary met us with the news that Jim's supervisor had given us the use of the conference room for the rest of the afternoon, "if we so wished." I recall being surprised and puzzled by this — what happened to the one-hour lunch break interview? And why?

The conference room was one of those plush, sound-proof rooms adorned with whiteboards, spare writing tablets, and continuous coffee service. It was a wonderfully luxurious place in which to talk, but totally unnecessary, maybe even inappropriate, and much too large for just Jim and me. At Jim's suggestion, we helped ourselves to coffee, picked two of the upholstered chairs at one end of the table and settled into a corner of the room which we were able to make seem rather cozy. Jim and I talked for the next two hours. While I often had to ask him to repeat things for me, I gradually got accustomed to his communication style and, with benefit of his facial expressions and body language, had less and less trouble understanding him.

> I'm the youngest of four kids. When I was one year old, the doctor told my parents to institutionalize me because I'd never walk or talk, would never know anything. It wasn't until I was 17 that they finally realized I wasn't retarded.
>
> But my mother knew all along I wasn't retarded and my parents refused to put me in an institution. I got speech, occupational and physical therapy and I was able to crawl. Doctors added weights to my body, which I carried around during the day, to slow my jerky movements and build up my muscles. I had wheels on my first walker and once I'd get going I'd make that thing fly. Eventually, they took the wheels off.
>
> I went to a school for the handicapped from when I was 6 to when I was 17. When I was working in a sheltered workshop, they had me supervising other people. But they were paying me the same sheltered workshop wages.

Because of his poor speech intelligibility, Jim's bright mind wasn't discovered until he was 17. As he sees it,

> Society looks at people who are blind or who use crutches and does not consider them to be mentally retarded. But they label people who have speech problems as mentally retarded.

When he was 17 he could not yet read or write and was placed in special education classes at his local high school. After just a few months, however, he was placed in regular classes because "Special Ed was just too easy."

After graduating from high school, Jim enrolled in a community college. Still unable to read, the frustrations of college landed him in the hospital. It was then that rehabilitation professionals got involved.

> I went into rehabilitation to learn to drive, but they said I first had to learn to feed myself. I resisted it, but in two weeks I was able to feed myself. They discovered that even though I'm right-handed, my left hand works better for feeding.
>
> I really came to believe that I can do the same things as everyone else, even though I may need more time. I learned to walk unaided at 10, to

read and feed myself at 19 and to drive a vehicle at 21. Maybe I learned later than most people how to do these things, but I did learn.

Rehabilitation gave me a tutor for reading and taught me how to drive. I dropped out of college, but I enrolled in a special program for the handicapped. Then I enrolled in another college for a degree in accounting.

Jim was one of thirty "handicapped but bright" individuals selected over a five-year time span for a special career training program that placed individuals for a year-long trial with appropriate employers. That was how Jim found his way to the insurance company, where he's been for the past four years.

This is a big step in my life... the final stretch of fitting into the career world. Walking out of the building with a suit on and carrying my work... and I'm just beginning.

I went back to Jim's office with him. As I was putting on my coat, Jim motioned for me to sit down and said,

You know, there were four of us boys basically alike at age 7. We were inseparable. One of them has died because he gave up. He got pneumonia from not wearing the right clothes for cold weather. Two are in sheltered workshops — and one of them can't handle his own finances and needs people to do everything for him.

I asked, "What do you think it is, Jim, that makes you so different from those other guys?"
He didn't have to think a second for his answer.

Encouragement... and courage. I was afraid I'd be alone someday. I have two parents and a brother and two sisters who would do anything for me, but they have their own lives. My parents treated us all the same and gave us a lot of encouragement. Once, to motivate me to be independent, they said, 'Hey, someday we're not going to be here.' That is reality.

I'm very glad I have my scooter and my van and my other aids. When you have a handicap, you need to find a new way of doing what you can't do by yourself. Parents and other caretakers will pass away. And there's a difference in being dependent on people or devices. People may or may not be there when you need them, but devices are still in the place where you last used them.

It's such a shame that...

Jim suddenly looked tired and there was a sadness in his eyes I hadn't seen before.

> ...that..well, devices don't have expectations, but people can have expectations that can hold you back.

PHYSICAL ASPECTS OF CEREBRAL PALSY

As with a spinal cord injury, a person with severe cerebral palsy can have a lifelong limitation in mobility because of paralysis. Cerebral palsy (CP) also results from injury — not to the spinal cord, but to the brain either before, during or after birth. Put together, the words "cerebral," meaning brain, and "palsy" or "motor disability" provide a verbal description of CP as a motor disability caused by a dysfunction in the brain. There are many different types of CP that vary according to the particular type of motor dysfunction: e.g. spasticity, athetosis, ataxia.[1] There are approximately 700,000 people in the U.S. who have CP and there are about 7,000 new cases per year (Condeluci, 1989).

Like spinal cord injuries, cerebral palsy can drastically reduce or totally curtail mobility and physical movements. But while people with CP and spinal cord injuries can share similar mobility dysfunctions, cerebral palsy is a "group of conditions." People with CP often have additional impairments because cerebral palsy affects people in more widely varying ways than do spinal cord injuries. As described by William Rush (1985), who has CP himself: "[CP] can leave a person with only a slight limp or it can leave a person unable to walk, talk, see and hear...Depending on the location and severity of the damage, cerebral palsy can also leave a person mentally competent or mentally retarded" (p. 27). Like a spinal cord injury, however, "it is not inherited, contagious, or terminal."

Cerebral palsy is a "developmental disability" which the Developmental Disabilities Act of 1984 (Public Law 98-527) defines as "severe, chronic conditions attributable to a mental or physical impairment, manifest before age 22, and likely to continue indefinitely, resulting in substantial limitations in a prescribed set of activities and requiring special interdisciplinary care" (Institute of Medicine, p. 109, 1991). Developmental Disabilities include people with mental retardation, cerebral palsy, Down Syndrome, epilepsy, autism, chronic illness and sensory impairment. According to the Institute of Medicine (1991), "an estimated 2 million to 4 million persons of all ages have such disabilities" (p. 109) and mental retardation and cerebral palsy are the two most common.

Dale Baum, author of *The Human Side of Exceptionality* (1982), notes that "For every 100,000 people born in one year, seven will have cerebral palsy. Of these seven:

1 will die in infancy,

2 of the remaining 6 will be mentally retarded and will require permanent custodial care, the remaining

4 will require medical and habilitation services, and finally, out of this group

1 may go to college" (p. 181).

It is interesting that Jim gave a similar breakdown for himself and his three seven-year-old friends.

Many Differences Can Exist Between Acquiring A Disability and Being Born With One

Jim's life history illustrates a major difference between a person with a *congenital disability* like cerebral palsy and someone like Chuck or Brian who acquired a disability in adulthood, known as becoming *adventitiously disabled*. Jim sees his assistive devices as having opened entirely new worlds to him and as keys to new experiences, opportunities and independence that would not have been possible without them. Jim has only experienced new-found capabilities. Unlike Chuck or Brian, he has not experienced functional loss with only a portion of previous functioning regained through the use of assistive technologies. When Jim goes into a restaurant with his friends from work, his feelings are very different from those of Chuck who was accustomed to walking in with friends before his accident and now feels patronized when with them in restaurants. Even though Brian is grateful for his van and being back on the road again, his gratitude doesn't compare to Jim's awe at being able to drive himself to and from work.

While Chuck and Brian also highly prize opportunity, independence, and new experiences, their assistive technologies represent compensation for what they can no longer do themselves. For them, a simple, low-tech device becomes a status symbol because it signifies both capability and ingenuity. Jim and other people with CP who use sophisticated high-tech devices, however, are usually perceived as having higher cognitive and linguistic abilities than CP users of simpler, low-tech, devices. Part of the status of high-tech device use comes from the belief that the CP user must be unusually endowed with financial resources and intelligence. In fact, the typical person with CP who is older than 30 years of age often does not have the social or educational background to take advantage of the opportunities of high-tech assistance. This person often appears under-educated and unsophisticated when compared to more advantaged peers or to the adventitiously disabled person who has experienced a so-called normal educational process.

Maggie provides an example of the value of some of the newer, high-tech devices for the older person with CP who has been educationally and socially advantaged. Because of her communication system, she has social and job opportunities now that she didn't before.

Maggie, 1986

I had been traveling and interviewing people all day. Feeling tired both emotionally and physically, the only thing I was thinking about was a quiet evening alone. However, when I reached my hotel room I noticed the message light on my phone flashing. The message was from Maggie, a person I was scheduled to interview the next day at the rehabilitation center. She was inquiring into the possibility of having our meeting that night at her mother's friend's apartment, since the next day she had to go apartment hunting and wouldn't be at the rehabilitation center. She had given me the phone number where she was staying and suggested a meeting time of 7 o'clock.

I looked at the clock and saw it was already 6:30 — where had the time gone? My decision was made instantly: If I didn't meet with Maggie tonight, chances were we wouldn't be able to get together again before I had to fly back. It was either tonight or not at all, and not-at-all was out of the question.

I called her to confirm our meeting and found out that Maggie had just been offered a job in another town, hence the need for her to go apartment-hunting. With a degree in social work, she was about to become a community services coordinator for an Independent Living Center. I ran a brush through my hair and headed outside to catch a cab. Twenty minutes later I was there.

As soon as I walked into the apartment I saw Maggie sitting in a battery-powered wheelchair so large it overpowered the apartment's living room. She was very excited about her job offer and her excitement made her spasticity very evident. Maggie struggled to speak — the end result of all her effort being a string of wordless sounds only decipherable by those familiar with her particular speech patterns.

Maggie's mother and her friend were there. Also, Maggie's companion and assistant, Theresa. Maggie and Theresa met several years before in a sheltered workshop. Theresa had been institutionalized for most of her life because of Down Syndrome[2], yet she drives, does all of the cooking, and is a good assistant for Maggie. While Maggie is very intelligent and has a college degree, she is extremely physically limited. Thus, she and Theresa have capabilities that so complement one another the needs of both are well met.

Maggie, 42, with severe (athetoid) cerebral palsy, is quadriparetic and has no discernible unaided speech. She communicates by using a manual communication board and is in the process of learning to use the Express III (computerized) communication system at the rehabilitation center.

Maggie's manual board is a very basic one with each letter of the alphabet and the numbers 0-9 enclosed in an individual box. Also housed in boxes were such key phrases as "please," "thank you," "I want," etc. Manual communication boards are highly individualized. Speech therapists adapt them to each individual's communication preferences. While Maggie's board contains letters, numbers, and phrases, other boards for non-verbal children or illiterate adults may have pictures or use the international Blissymbolics (a pictographic, meaning-based, system of twenty-six basic symbols that can be superimposed on one another to form an infinite number of concepts and combined to form sentences). A manual communication board user, or sender, points to a symbol (a letter, word, number or picture) with a finger or some other type of pointer. The custom followed by receivers is to repeat out loud the entire message as it has been understood. This tells the board user that the message has or has not been understood accurately. With an affirmative head nod, the user acknowledges accurate understanding. A negative head nod immediately followed by continued pointing indicates clarification is in process.

I had hoped to see Maggie's Express III in action, and was disappointed to learn she was keeping it at the rehabilitation center during her training. Thus, her means of communication tonight was to be the manual board.

The use of a manual communication board is tedious for both the user and receiver, as I was to experience that evening with Maggie. The temptation is always great for the parent or friend to jump in and finish sentences for the belabored speaker. Maggie, in order to prevent just such a thing from happening, had asked to meet with me alone so that her responses wouldn't be "interpreted," as she put it. However, all five of us ended up sitting around the kitchen table and for three hours we watched Maggie slowly and arduously spell out her responses to my questions, seeing her resort to abbreviations and shorthand ways of getting her message across.

A typical exchange would go something like this:

"Tell me, Maggie, what is the biggest advantage of the Express III over this board?"

"They have voice in computer."

When I asked Maggie for her definition of a "rehabilitation success" she replied:

"Me."

Further probing led into her perception of her quality of life, which she described as:

"Good because I am determined."

"Is there anything that would make it better?"

"I would like more of a social life."

After a short break of cake and coffee, we resumed our pace. Towards the end, her obvious physical exhaustion, coupled with everyone's general fatigue, caused all of us to jump in to try and finish Maggie's words and thoughts for her. It was becoming a game of "Twenty Questions" but Maggie didn't even mind anymore. Thus it was obviously time to end the interview.

Without a background of quality social and educational experiences, many congenitally-disabled individuals (those with cerebral palsy being just one example) would not be given the same opportunities as Maggie. They often live at or below the poverty line and their lack of financial resources, coupled with their lack of sophistication about high-tech assistive devices, result in situations where they not only can't afford devices, but might not understand the fundamentals of their operation. Thus, they can very easily become stuck in a state of perpetual and permanent deprivation.

Communication Technologies are World-Openers — Sometimes

Christopher Nolan, the Irish poet/author who has cerebral palsy, cannot produce intelligible sounds, cannot walk, and can voluntarily control only nods of his head. In his autobiography (1987), he describes how he felt being able to use a typewriter at age 11 to express his thoughts and ideas. With his mother steadying his head so that he could apply a pointer to the typewriter keyboard, he "typed beauty from within, beauty of secret knowledge so secretly hidden and so nearly lost forever" (Nolan, p. 56, 1987). Some years later, a computer scientist worked with him on the use of a word processor, which he describes as follows:

> With the alphabet upon the screen and the cursor hopping along from one letter to the next, all [I] had to do now was strike [my] chin against a nearly placed switch and miracle of miracles, the letter would appear in a boxed-off area of the screen. There and then disability would be conquered. Conscious of the greatness in that movement by which [I] struck the chin-switch, [I] waited for the green cursor to come to the required letter, but by that time [my] acute mind had foreseen the difficulty, [my] entire body froze rigid, and [my] eyes watched the cursor hop by... The next time was the same, and the next...[On the next attempt I] made a wallop at the switch which almost beheaded me... (p.83-84).

The stories of Jim, Maggie and Christopher Nolan (and countless un-named others) highlight several facts: Without the means to access communication devices, typewriters or word processors, a brilliant mind can be a secret "nearly lost forever." But some means are more produc-tive than others. Computer technology may not be the most efficient answer for all individuals with severe cerebral palsy. For example, Jim prefers not to use his "inefficient" communication device that cannot keep up with the fast pace around his office. Christopher Nolan had been doing very well with the typewriter as long as he had someone to steady his head.

Computerized communication systems, which includes VOCAS (voice output communication aids) are much more complex and sophis-ticated means of communication than manual communication boards. They require considerable training and can be very frustrating — if one can afford to obtain one in the first place. Users need to have high cognitive abilities, a fondness of computers, and a tolerance for looking and sounding somewhat "automated." The following paragraphs describe the Express I, the first member of the Express family. The updated Express III (the system Maggie was in the process of learning) differs primarily in its synthesized voice output capability.

> The Express communication system, manufactured by Prentke-Romich Company, is a small computer activated by one of a variety of switches (a joystick, a mouthstick, an arm-slot control, a manual pointer, an optical headpointer) and through any part of the body the user can control — head, tongue, chin, shoulder, knee, even a puff of breath. Direct selection can be gained to all the board's capabilities by directly touching a square on the board's matrix with a finger or a pointer. *Indirect access* can be accomplished with a joystick that remotely controls a light spot on the board which scans in any direction until the desired square is reached. The joy-stick method takes a little longer, but it accomplishes the task with no more than gross movement.
>
> The slowest process, again providing indirect access to the board, is *row-column scanning* accessed by paddle, wobble or puff/sip switches. The operator hits the switch once to make the scanner start. The light spot then goes line by line until the operator makes it stop at the desired square by hitting the switch again.
>
> The Express can store on four different levels the same kinds of words, phrases and symbols used on a manual board. Once the user accesses a square, the selection appears in a display box at the top of the device. Spelling or wording can be changed, and words can be connected into sentences before they are printed out or spoken through the voice synthesizer.
>
> The Express III is designed to accept a variety of peripherals and attachments such as a video display for a television screen, an automatic telephone, and, through an environmental control unit, any electrical appliance. It can be connected to a personal computer and, thus, to all of the workday and leisure applications a home computer offers (Summers and Joslyn-Scherer, 1982).

People with severe cerebral palsy can now become employed, like Jim and Maggie, and can even become world-renowned prize-winning writers, like Christopher Nolan. And, thanks to medical and technical advances, their careers can be long ones.

This is an especially exciting time for today's children with cerebral palsy. The congenitally disabled person 30 years of age or older, however, represents a transition between two worlds: The pre-technology and pre-civil rights world of relative segregation and deprivation, and the high-tech world of enhanced capabilities and newly gained opportunities. Traversing through such a transition can be difficult — even perilous.

REFERENCE NOTES

[1]   Depending on the area of the central nervous system affected, cases of cerebral palsy are categorized as spastic, athetoid and ataxic. The New York State Senate Select Subcommittee on the Disabled (1989) defines spasticity, athetosis, and ataxia as follows:

1. *Spasticity.* Spasticity is the most common type of Cerebral Palsy. It is found in about 50 to 60% of cases, mostly with hemiplegia (paralysis of one side of the body) or less likely, with quadriplegia (total paralysis of the body from the neck down). The muscle tone is increased, and there is increased resistance to passive movement. When the muscles are stretched, as in attention to movement, there is an increased stretch reflex and the muscle contracts strongly, involuntarily and inaccurately. The person walks with a characteristic "scissor gait."

2. *Athetosis.* Athetosis is a type of Cerebral Palsy found in approximately 20 to 25 percent of children with CP. Purposeful movements are contorted and the person has abnormal posturing and uncontrollable and uncoordinated jerky, twisting movements of the extremities. The head is often drawn back with the mouth open. In trying to talk, the person may grimace. Ability to walk may vary according to circumstances, perhaps improving when the person is not anxious and is well rested.

3. *Ataxia.* This is a rather uncommon type of Cerebral Palsy, varying between one to 15 percent of the population of persons with CP. The person has a disturbed sense of balance and has a greatly decreased ability to maintain balance or coordination. The person may exhibit a high stepping gait and may stumble, lurch and fall easily. Nystagmus (involuntary rapid eye movement) and tremor of the head may be seen.

Many individuals with severe CP have a combination of the above characteristics.

2   In 1854, Dr. Langdon Down described a certain group of people according to the following common characteristics: eyes that slope at the outer corners, the impression of a broad flat face, small stubby hands, shorter physique and smaller head. People with Down Syndrome look so similar to one another that it seems they must all be siblings. The majority of individuals with Down Syndrome are at least slightly retarded.

In 1959, it was discovered that the cause of Down Syndrome is an extra chromosome — 47 instead of the normal 46.

CHAPTER THREE

In God We Trust[1]: A Brief Historical Review of Rehabilitation Practices

> The past is a foreign country:
> they do things differently there.
> L.P. Hartley (in the Prologue to *The Go-Between*)

The time in which Chuck, Brian, Jim and Maggie live is like no other in U.S. history for persons with disabilities. Their constitutional right to Life has come to be as much a guarantee of advances in technology, medicine and rehabilitation as it has human rights. They have the Liberty to pursue all forms of Happiness. Yet it is perhaps nowhere else more apparent than in the study of the history of the care and treatment of people with disabilities that there has been over time a waxing and waning in America's guarantees of freedom, equality, justice, and humanity.

It is important when discussing the treatment of and attitudes toward persons with disabilities to realize that these do not occur in a vacuum — they are part of the complex and dynamic social, political, economic, and technological emphases at a particular point in time. To provide a context, this chapter provides highlights of the different "epochs" in our history to show how we have evolved over the past 200+ years into a society that passes such legislation as the *Americans with Disabilities Act*, *Technology Related Assistance for Individuals with Disabilities Act* and *Individuals with Disabilities Education Act* while continuing to segregate students in our schools and protest the establishment of group homes in our neighborhoods.

AMERICA DURING THE AGRICULTURAL OR PRE-INDUSTRIAL AGE

In the first century after the signing of the Constitution, at least 45% of Americans lived on farms. Before automobiles and systems of rapid transit, the exchange of goods and services across a broad area could not be readily accomplished. Farms were self-sufficient systems for life sustenance.

In pre-industrial America, Chuck and Brian would not have survived their injuries. Had Jim and Maggie lived on farms, they would have been cared for by family members, perhaps with help from friends and neighbors. If it had been decided that they needed more care than these persons could provide, they would have been sent to special institutions established for their "treatment" — treatment that amounted to ware-housing, less than proper care and feeding. For example, a Philadelphian in the early 1700's could, for a shilling, go to the Pennsylvania Hospital and, in the casual manner the antics of zoo animals are observed today, watch the "bizarre behaviors" exhibited by the men and women chained to the damp, dark basement walls.

In 1813, Philadelphia Quakers took a bold step against the chain-and-shackle treatment of mentally ill individuals by placing them in a country setting where they were free to walk the grounds and work in the gardens. Thus was founded the first private psychiatric hospital in the U.S., known as the Friends Asylum for the Relief of Persons Deprived of the Use of Their Reason (later renamed the Friends Hospital).

By and large, however, the farm metaphor of tending to and watch-ing over the herd of livestock, sheltering them en masse in the barn, was frequently a fitting one for the kind of care given persons with disabilities in the early nineteenth century. The dominant institutional pattern was isolation or segregation from non-impaired populations. Institutionali-zation was based on the assumption that the removal of certain popula-tions from public life served the needs of both society and persons with disabilities, as the latter were increasingly perceived as requiring a level of supervision beyond which a family or small network of friends and neighbors could provide.

Institutions were typically located in sparsely populated areas, remote from public observance and supervision. Since the facts of what com-prised contagious diseases were little understood or known, and there were not yet effective disease control mechanisms, people with such varying conditions as cerebral palsy, epilepsy, leprosy, and tuberculosis were sent to large public institutions in isolated regions of the U.S. and, essentially, "quarantined" physically and socially. High walls surround-ing the institution and massive gates served to control institutional entry and departure. Access within the institutions was often controlled by locked doors. Even private institutions for the wealthy sick were established in remote locations, as much to control contact as to maintain secrecy and preserve the anonymity of the elite clientele.

The average citizen, thus, did not need to be concerned directly with the Jims and Maggies of the time, that segment of the population labeled chronically ill or disabled. Institutions also served to legitimize the belief that the segregation of persons with disabilities from the rest of society was appropriate and necessary, and that the responsibility for responding to the special needs of disabled persons was a matter for professionals and other individuals especially employed to be their caretakers.

Within the walls of the institutions themselves, custodial care was seen as a practical response to the hopeless circumstances of nonexistent cures and almost certain death. To ensure control of both employees and residents, routinized caretaking became a necessity. Institutionalized behavior became the outcome of routinized and institutionalized care. The inadequate stimulation given to persons with disabilities invariably resulted in life-long dependence and low levels of functioning. In many cases individuals with cerebral palsy were thought to be mentally retarded when, in fact, they had normal intelligence upon admission to the institution but had failed to develop. After some period in the institution, they often had deteriorated in cognitive and social skills because of the sparse stimulation of the institutional environment.

The idea of returning people to their communities as psychosocially and vocationally prepared to resume productive roles in society had yet to take hold. The concept of rehabilitation was primarily limited to hospitals providing prosthetic limbs and to schools for the education of individuals with serious visual and/or hearing impairments, delinquent boys, and persons with epilepsy. In 1848, the Fernald School opened in Boston dedicated to the rehabilitation of those with mental retardation. While these institutions were begun with agendas that stressed rehabilitation most soon deteriorated into institutions resembling the "poorhouse". (see Michael B. Katz (1968), and Schwartz (1992).

EARLY INDUSTRIAL AMERICA

Man as a Machine

During pre-industrial America and the early years of the Industrial Age, the majority of any given day was devoted to home maintenance, family and farm sustenance. Household appliances and farming tools, though mechanically very simple by today's standards, did much to help to reduce the workload. Early sewing machines, food grinders, and clothes wringers sparked as much affection for machines by those who worked in the home as the steam engine and cotton gin did for those who worked the land. Newly available mechanical devices and assistance were enthusiastically sought out by consumers and eagerly created by occasionally overzealous inventors.

More was becoming known about machines than about human anatomy. While more and more people were being intimately exposed to the machine, few were privy to the inner workings of their own bodies. As medicine began to advance and Newtonian physics was being adopted as a world view, the analogy of the machine was often used to explain the mysteries of bodily structures, processes, and functions. Man came to be seen as composed of a set of mechanisms. This served both to mechanize humankind and to humanize machines.

Machines came to be seen as viable replacements for weak or missing parts of the human anatomy. More sophisticated braces for arms, legs, and backs were being forged. After the Civil War, prosthetic arms, hands, and legs were being crafted that appear crude by today's standards, but were actually vast technical improvements. Large numbers of manual wheelchairs, called "invalid rolling chairs," were being produced as well.

In 1850, the U.S. population was 23 million. Twenty-five years later it had doubled. Railroads and tunnels were helping to link persons and towns. Man's mastery over nature and machine appeared certain and the young industrial society was based on the well-accepted premise that the machine and the factory represented the most advanced and efficient means to meet the burgeoning demand for produced goods. The factory, to be highly productive, had to be as well-oiled as the machine. Predictability, reliability, repeatability and synchronization were considered crucial for maximum efficiency in mass production. These buzz words of the day were applied to human performance and behavior as well — performance standards people like Jim or Maggie were hardly equipped to meet.

There were large numbers of people who could not compete in our newly industrialized society without services to help restore function physically, mentally, emotionally, and socially. With the dawning of the

Industrial Age and the movement of many families from farms to the cities, the response to people like Jim or Maggie was to ignore their needs and to exclude them from societal participation. Religious and other charitable organizations founded institutions, schools, and centers for disabled persons, but in the absence of national standards and guidelines, the quality of care varied widely. The gap between need and response to that need was indeed very wide.

Man is a Machine

One hundred years ago, the Industrial Revolution was in full swing. The need for labor to run the machines and factories was great, so America was quite hospitable to young and healthy immigrants from across the Atlantic Ocean. To all approaching the shores of New York City, the Statue of Liberty proclaimed America a haven for "...your tired, your poor, your huddled masses yearning to breathe free, the wretched refuse of your teeming shore..." while many *poor* American citizens were considered to be *wretched refuse* to be set aside in isolated institutions.

Yet, there were some who held out great humanitarian hopes for the Industrial Age and machines in the late 1800's. Futurist utopian writers like Edward Bellamy in *Looking Backward* wrote about late 19th century society as a time of "unexampled intellectual splendor and of mechanical inventions, scientific discovery, art, musical and literary productiveness to which no previous age of the world offers anything comparable." He characterized future society as stable and prosperous with a universal reign of brotherhood, jobs for everyone, people wanting for nothing and a public spirit that had overcome all selfishness. He saw us as a society of perfect harmony and envisioned a virtual elimination of privilege and servants, crime, war, insanity and suicide.

Bellamy's socialist writing was done in a time when the rift between the rich and the poor was growing dramatically. As such, he believed that diversity and individuality leads to individual distress and social discontent.

While Bellamy was writing, factories were becoming huge organizational hierarchies with class divisions. Specialization and standardization, which emphasized uniformity and conformity, became the work order of the day. Scientific and technical knowledge were more highly regarded than particular job skills.

20TH CENTURY AMERICA

Necessity — and wars — have been the mothers of invention for many things, including rehabilitation services. One of the many events to greatly change the essentially custodial services to services emphasizing *rehabilitation* was World War I. With many soldiers returning without limbs, sight, or hearing, the Soldier's Rehabilitation Act was passed in 1918 to provide vocational retraining of disabled veterans. Soon thereafter, in the heat of debates and concerns about labor union demands for rehabilitation services for workers, the Vocational Rehabilitation Act of 1920 (Public Law 236) extended the same vocational benefits to civilians. This federal support was annually renewed until 1935, when rehabilitation achieved permanent status under legislative amendments to the Social Security Act. Rehabilitation services were initially provided only to the "physically disabled."

The debut of the antibiotic drugs, sulfa and penicillin between the mid-thirties and early forties enabled medical professionals to halt many viral and post-operative infections. This, coupled with advances in casualty and trauma management learned on the war's battlefields, allowed significantly more people than ever before to survive major illnesses and injuries with some form of permanent limitation or disability.

When American factories began to lose their workers to World War II battlefields, they hired women, minority workers, and individuals with disabilities to operate the machines and supply the war effort. Women discovered that machines had made it possible for many household tasks to be done more efficiently. They no longer needed to devote full-time effort to home maintenance. Women, minority workers, and workers with disabilities found employment opportunities in wartime industries to be very attractive and they did not want to relinquish their jobs to returning veterans. Emerging from the war as a victorious and prosperous society, post-war America could afford to be committed to both returning veterans and their replacement workers. In possession of the resources to become a more humane society, the United States entered a period of economic and social expansion.

Skyscrapers, suspension bridges, streamlined locomotives, airplanes, airports, automobiles, an interstate network of concrete highways and service stations were inspiring symbols of unprecedented human well-being. The appearance of television sets in middle-class homes in the early 1950's, the launch of Sputnik in 1957, the invention of the transistor and the first Xerox copier in 1958, all signalled a new epoch in communication and the increasing role of electronics. The mass production and transportation of consumer goods heralded the growth of a consumer-oriented society. While machines of that post-World War II era tend now to call forth images of grey, dirty factories and pollution, machines had become the all-encompassing world-wide symbol of progress and prosperity. Machines also embodied the dominant motif vocationally and socially.

Individuals disabled after World War II, around the time Maggie was born, had the benefit of great advances made possible by the Industrial Revolution and by important developments in the concept of rehabilitation engendered by treating the casualties of World War II. The enactment of the Vocational Rehabilitation Act Amendments of 1943 (Public Law 113) had increased state vocational services and the funds needed to provide those services. Medical, surgical, and other physically restorative services were added to the concept of rehabilitation, and those with mental illness were determined to be eligible for rehabilitation services. The numbers of persons with disabilities were increasing substantially, and so too were the numbers being served in rehabilitation facilities during this period.

Rehabilitation mandates continued to expand through federal legislation. By the time Jim was born in 1957, the Department of Health, Education and Welfare was four years old and Public Law 565 (authorizing a nationwide system of training grants to increase the supply of rehabilitation personnel) had been in existence for three years. P.L. 565 also made grant monies available to help fund research into the issues related to disabling conditions and to test and model new approaches to rehabilitation. It provided the funds for the states to establish community rehabilitation programs. In 1954 another act provided badly needed construction monies for rehabilitation facilities. In 1965, the most liberal and far-reaching piece of national legislation on behalf of persons with disabilities was passed. That legislation, Public Law 333 established behavioral disabilities and cultural and economic deprivation as handicapping conditions in need of rehabilitation services. Sheltered workshops, rehabilitation facilities, and self-help programs were encouraged or expanded.

The Sixties was a very socially conscious decade. The Kennedy years and Johnson's Great Society brought the Peace Corps, VISTA, and the

War on Poverty. A concern for equal human rights peaked in the early and mid-1960's. Ten years after the 1954 Supreme court decision against segregated education in Brown vs. the Board of Education of Topeka, Kansas, Congress passed the Civil Rights Act (Title VI) in 1964 which ended segregation. Almost a decade later, the word "black" in the Civil Rights Act was replaced by the words "disabled individuals" and civil rights were extended to individuals with disabilites under Section 504 of the Vocational Rehabilitation Amendments of 1973. Anti-discrimination laws based on sex and age were also passed based on the Civil Rights Act.

During this period of civil rights and humanitarian concerns, the needs of large numbers of people who could benefit from rehabilitation services became a focus and growth for rehabilitation resources and facilities was legislated. With the newly created Social and Rehabilitation Service in 1967, rehabilitation leaders were able to successfully advocate and obtain significantly broadened services for people with disabilities. They encouraged new productive alliances and relationships among a host of public and private agencies and organizations. Community rehabilitation programs and facilities sprang up by the hundreds, with widespread citizen support and involvement.

They Were Very Good Years

Due to the favorable political and civil rights climates in the '60s and '70s, laws were passed to ensure the equality and humanity guaranteed 200 hundred years before in the Constitution and the Bill of Rights.

In addition to Section 504, which provided individuals with equal access to programs and services, and non-discrimination in education and employment, many other legislative acts and governmental efforts extended rights to Americans with disabilities: The Rehabilitation Act Amendments of 1974 and 1978, the National Housing Act Amendments in 1975, the Education for All Handicapped Children Act of 1975 (Public Law 94-142), the 1977 White House Conference on Handicapped Individuals, the Social Security Disability Amendments of 1980, and the designation of 1982-1992 as the international "Decade of Disabled Persons."

Many professional organizations began to devote significant energies to improving the status of professionals with disabilities. Some examples:

- the American Association for the Advancement of Science (AAAS) would hold scientists with disabilities up as role models;

- the Special Interest Group on Computer Assistance for the Physically Handicapped (SIGCAPH) would annually select the "outstanding handicapped federal employee."

These private and public efforts changed the look of American cities and towns:

- thousands of ramps were built,
- notices in Braille were posted,
- traffic lights might use sounds to indicate *stop* and *walk*,
- handicapped parking spaces were more widely available,
- wheelchair accessible toilets become commonplace, and
- teletypewriters for persons with hearing impairments were installed.

These also had the cumulative effect of generating much hope and optimism about the future quality of life for people with disabilities.

Rehabilitation was redefined to mean not just the recently enhanced ability to restore function, but the restoration of dignity to the lives of people with physical disabilities. Services were designed to assist individuals in returning to their communities so they could live independently and exercise as many free choices as possible. With institutionalization fast going out of favor, a tiered community-based system was adopted where foster family placements, group residences, and supervised apartments were the residential options.

In 1970 in Berkeley, California, a group of students with disibilities moved out of the campus hospital (which was their dormitory) and into the community. They saw the real issues facing people with disabilities as being not medical, but political and economic, e.g., access to transportation, housing, personal assistance, and jobs. People with disabilities, the former students believed, should help other people with disabilities; those who have been through the experience know best how others might achieve independence. Working together, people with disabilities can attain self-direction and manage their own programs. Thus was born the Independent Living Movement. The Rehabilitation Act Amendments of 1978 furthered the movement by fostering the establishment of Independent Living Centers throughout the U.S.

People riding in wheelchairs and modified vans, those walking city streets with guide dogs, burst out from behind closed doors and began to advocate for themselves and form coalitions and self-help organizations.[2] People with disabilities were encouraged by the rehabilitation system and the 1977 White House Conference on Handicapped Individuals to "assume more responsibility for intermixing on a social level, eliminating unnecessary dependence on able-bodied persons, and speaking out on issues" (p. 36) and such slogans as "fall down and be counted" and "label jars, not people" were proudly sounded. They also were told, "Only by consistent recognition of the problems faced by persons with disabilities because of public attitudes, and only through an ongoing effort to change those attitudes, can progress be made toward equality of all people" (p. 136). Thus, "The handicapped should be visible in the community to help the general public better understand the additional needs of the handicapped and activities required by the handicapped" (p.31).

Large numbers of people with disabilities were now encountering one another daily throughout America's communities. They started by actively working together in their own advocacy groups for a better quality of life through equal rights and accessibility. Before this time, advocacy group activities were run as charities by able-bodied individuals who would solicit contributions on behalf of persons with disabilities for medical research and rehabilitation programs (e.g. current ones include the Lions Club campaigns on behalf of persons with visual impairments and blindness; Jerry Lewis' work for his "kids" with muscular dystrophy). The newer groups, run by individuals with disabilities themselves, became heavily engaged in political lobbying and the development of public awareness programs.

As people with a variety of physical disabilities began to zealously appear in communities across the U.S., there was a need for more and better assistive devices. There was and is an interactive relationship among many aspects of community (re)integration of people with disabilities and technological advances. That is, since assistive devices further independence and community integration, increased community acceptance and inclusion of people with disabilities requires continuous attention to device creation, design and modification.

Also, progress in one area highlights unmet needs in others. For example, independent mobility by battery-powered wheelchair required there be accessible buildings and modified transportation systems; the Americans With Disabilities Act of 1990, which extends to individuals with physical and mental disabilities "reasonable accommodations" of individual needs, and the Individuals with Disabilities Education Act (IDEA) of 1990, which encourages the consideration of assistive technologies in each relevant IEP, (Individualized Education Plan) closely followed the passage of the Technology-Related Assistance for Individuals with Disabilities Act of 1988. Figures 3-1 & 3-2 show the inter-relationships among these recent laws and the social/political climate in which they were enacted.

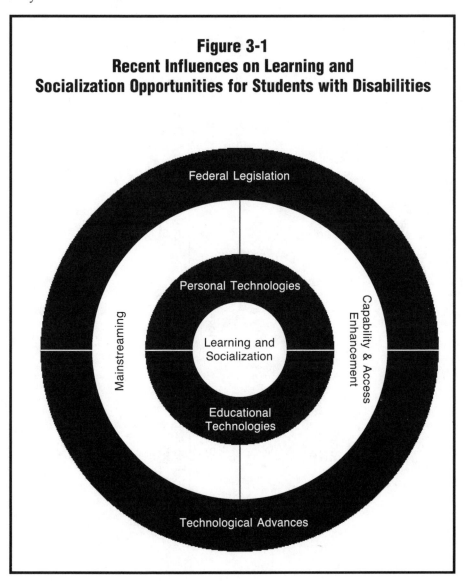

**Figure 3-1
Recent Influences on Learning and
Socialization Opportunities for Students with Disabilities**

Figure 3-2
Socio-political Events

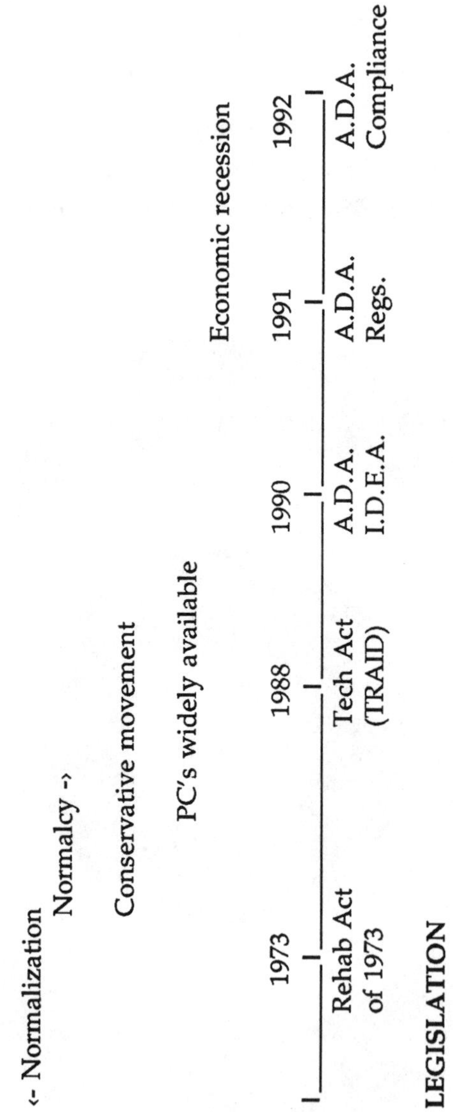

<- Normalization

Normalcy ->

Conservative movement

PC's widely available

Economic recession

1973	1988	1990	1991	1992
Rehab Act of 1973	Tech Act (TRAID)	A.D.A. I.D.E.A.	A.D.A. Regs.	A.D.A. Compliance

LEGISLATION

FROM THE INDUSTRIAL TO THE INFORMATION AGE

Machines and technology made it possible to mass produce many of the major components of assistive devices which together with the invention of the microprocessor in the mid-1970's, made it possible for devices to be smaller, more portable and less expensive. This, in turn, made assistive devices more affordable and they became more widely available. A physical limitation was no longer something that needed to prevent a person from participating in and contributing to society. Vocational rehabilitation counselors were knocking more frequently on employers' doors and those doors were opening.

Assistive devices made possible by machines and advanced technology helped to equalize the functioning of persons with and without a disability. People with disabilities began to believe that a shift would occur from an emphasis on impairment to one on intact abilities and that the image of the passive and dependent disabled person would give way to one of competence and self-reliance.

While persons with physical disabilities were singing technology's praises, former patients of psychiatric institutions were actively protesting the use of machines and electricity in their treatment and rehabilitation. The availability of such technologically advanced assistive devices as battery-powered wheelchairs and equipment to modify vans made it possible for people with physical disabilities to be more independent and to integrate more in the community. Technology to them represented progress and opportunity. To many former psychiatric patients who underwent electroconvulsive or "shock" therapy, however, technology represented *loss* (particularly of memory), limitation of future opportunities, and even torturous punishment. And many worried that individuals with mental retardation and other cognitive disabilities would be further handicapped by an emphasis on computer and information processing skills. Differing perspectives of technology is just one area among many that serves to drive a wedge into the disabled community, separating those with physical from those with mental, emotional, or cognitive disabilities.

CAD: Computer-Assisted Dreaming

The Industrial Revolution spawned needs that people wanted to have met earlier, faster, and better. Automobiles and jets made daily travel commonplace. National and international businesses developed with unprecedented speed. The demand for prompt global information from newspapers, television, and radio was great. The race to control information was on.

One hundred years after the cotton gin was invented, Diesel patented the first combustion engine in 1892. In another fifty years the U.S. saw the debut of the first "automatic computer" in 1942. Today, fifty years later, the home and office personal computer is commonplace, hundreds of satellites circle the globe bringing us instant worldwide communication, and microwave ovens cook our meals in mere minutes.

America has moved very rapidly from a manufacturing, machine-dominated society to a thinking, information-driven one. Where oil and iron were the icons of the Industrial Age, the computer is the new and idealized symbol of the Information Age. Americans became enthralled with computerized factories and offices, telecommunications, electronic banking, computer-based instruction, and high-tech medicine and rehabilitation. Where the heart had been said to work "like a pump," we began to hear "a stroke results from overloaded circuitry." Computer terminology replaced the language of the factory and of Freudian psychology for describing our behaviors; the ego had turned into "the operating system."

People were computerized and computers were humanized. Human beings could now be composed of computer-like components (for example, pacemakers) and have life itself maintained by high-tech systems such as kidney dialysis and artificial respiration. Machine and human parts were suddenly interchangeable.

When personal computers became widely available in the early 1980's, electronic management of just about everything was literally within fingertip reach. Persons with severe physical disabilities were able to activate their powered wheelchairs with nothing more than a head nod, as Chuck does, and those without intelligible speech, like Maggie, could finally express their thoughts by means of a computer with synthesized speech output. As machines and computers kept getting smaller and more portable, there seemed to be no constraints on dreams of complete freedom and unlimited opportunity.

Lean Times and a Renewed Push Towards "Normality"

By 1985, closing in on the middle of the Decade of Disabled Persons, the rosy picture that had been painted just a decade before was rapidly fading. The political, economic, and social climates had changed and optimism declined for an improved quality of life for persons with disabilities. Watergate made people distrustful of the government and governmental programs and interventions came to be equated with undesirable intrusion into the private lives of American individuals. Accountability was the buzz word of the day and a conservative mood swept the country. Hard-won civil and equal rights slowly eroded.

Government-sponsored programs were cutting back services due to a shortage of available funds. Rehabilitation units in hospitals found they had to push people out faster or lose money. The private sector, too, faced the need to trim programs. Those individuals who wanted or needed more long-term, intensive rehabilitation found themselves in the uncomfortable position of needing to establish their own fund-raising campaigns. Such individuals and their families began to air their appeals through the media and send out form letters soliciting funds.[3] Families and individuals already emotionally taxed by the occurrence and management of a disability now also felt degraded.

Whereas the overarching philosophy guiding rehabilitation policy in the '70s was **normalization**, the 1980's philosophy became a push towards **normality**. **Normalization** held that people with disabilities could be helped to exhibit personal, social, and work behaviors as close to **normal** as possible and they should be treated no differently from anyone else. Social institutions were expected to adapt situations so these persons could function as part of the mainstream. Without denying the presence of a disability, proponents of normalization worked for the elimination of special treatment and privileges and gave birth to such ideas as educational mainstreaming. **Normality**, on the other hand, implied that disabled persons would actively strive to function as if they had no disability at all. Until that could be accomplished, proponents of normality advocated "separate but equal" mainstreaming opportunities where disabled children would be given the same education as other children, but in separate classrooms.

Some mainstreaming opportunities have always existed, but only since the late 1970's and early 1980's have significant numbers of disabled American students been exposed to integrated educational settings. People with disabilities in mainstreamed schools today are exposed to more varied role models and stricter educational standards than were present in the institutions and segregated specialized settings. They are growing up under different expectations than those older than themselves, like Jim and Maggie, who did not have mainstreaming opportunities. Thus, in this time of great transition, people of different ages among those with disabilities have led comparatively different lives. The young, malleable individual with a disability preparing for life in the 21st century experiences a less confining life style and may be using assistive technologies early in school. They may or may not have contacts with older and more seasoned persons with disabilities.

The promise of **normality** is deceptive. As will become apparent, many individuals understand their expanded capabilities are due to these recent dramatic changes, but they feel very keenly the remaining limits their disability imposes — especially socially and in long-term personal relationships. Thus, issues of self-worth and identity are often just as confusing as ever.

The hope behind the flurry of activity in normalization, mainstreaming, and the Independent Living Movement was that the quality of life for *all* persons with disabilities would vastly improve so they would have the same opportunities and resources as non-disabled persons. While the institutions were empty, the moral equivalent of institutionalization and "quarantine" — stigma — continued to exist. The results of a survey conducted for the International Center for the Disabled in 1986 showed disabled Americans still to be less educated and poorer than non-disabled Americans. More than half of the survey respondents reported they feel "their disability has prevented them from reaching their full abilities as a person." (p. 4)

This survey of 1,000 Americans with disabilities, however, in trying to fairly represent all age groups, included the educational and employment experiences of older persons. Since older people with disabilities have not experienced the same opportunities for education and rehabilitation as younger individuals (even people Jim's age) who have recently gone through the system, it is not surprising they found younger persons with disabilities to be more frequently employed and better educated.

The Glory Days of Mainstreaming Wane

The shift in focus from *manufacturing* to *information management* made individuals with cognitive, behavioral, and social deficits especially disadvantaged. In 1985, ten years after the mainstreaming act was passed, articles appeared in such journals as *Exceptional Children* extolling the vices of mainstreaming. People observed that being in integrated classrooms and being compared against the performance of non-disabled students had negative consequences such as stifled initiative, and peer rejection emanating from differences in communication and social skills.

Undeniably, socialization deficits could be found in students with disabilities. Due to transportation and other problems of accessibility, these students often do not have as many opportunities as most non-disabled students to learn and practice a large repertoire of social skills in naturalistic settings with peers. Like Jim and Maggie, they typically haven't been exposed to a wide variety of people and places.

Critics pointed out that when mainstreamed, on the other hand, many students with disabilities were without frequent opportunities to talk with others having similar disabilities to share ideas and experiences. Without this sharing, it can be especially difficult to establish a firm identity.

It is widely believed in the field of deaf education, for example, that mainstreamed educational experiences enhance a deaf person's English and communication abilities. The students who are well-adjusted personally, however, are those from residential schools for the deaf where they have been educationally segregated from hearing students but have grown up with abundant opportunities to make friends with age mates and older students who are also hearing impaired.

The passage of the Individuals with Disabilities Education Act (IDEA) of 1990 mandates the consideration of assistive device use in each relevant "individualized education plan" (IEP.) This law, along with others recently passed, may help assure that the students entering our public schools today will have an educational career that is both academically and socially rewarding.

In education, and elsewhere, the history of the United States shows that public support for assimilating people with disabilities into mainstream America has waxed and waned. Now, as we go into the 21st Century, persons with disabilities still face the need to temper their optimism. For example, the Americans with Disabilities Act (A.D.A.) is being implemented during an economic recession when companies are down-sizing, and there are no funds available for the provision of reasonable job accommodations and assistive technologies. In early January, 1992 the *Wall Street Journal* reported that President Bush was considering placing a moratorium on A.D.A. until key economic indicators pointed to an impending economic recovery.

As one person with a disability has noted, "Our civil rights are like muscles — the more we exercise them, the more they'll develop and what you don't use you'll lose (Dragona, 1985, p.35). The shifts in the economic health of the nation notwithstanding, civil liberties are fragile. They are highly vulnerable to those who find certain rights and liberties person- ally offensive (e.g. the freedom to be a street-corner preacher), dangerous to public health and safety (e.g. mandated use of seat belts) and detrimen- tal to moral order (e.g. the debate over legalized abortion).

Our experiences with mechanization and then computerization have made us a society accustomed to rapid change, transition and its atten- dant confusion. From these changes may come an enhanced tolerance and respect for all individuals' human rights. In the meantime, who can help but be impressed by Brian's accomplishments in college — and on the ski slope? And can it be any wonder that Jim is awed by and grateful for the opportunity to walk out of his office building with a suit on and carrying his work?

REFERENCE NOTES

[1]   There are many excellent sources one can turn to for an understand- ing of the history of rehabilitation in America. The reference materials used to write this chapter, listed in the "Reference" section at the end of the book, are good representations of the available literature in this area.

[2]   The oldest self-help organization in the United States is the National Association for the Deaf (NAD), founded in 1880.

[3]   In August, 1991 the author received the following letter. Except for the removal of identifying information, it is printed in it's entirety.

[address]
[phone number]
August 12, 1991

Tom, our 23 year old son, was involved in an auto accident in January, 1991. The result was a spinal cord injury which left him a quadriplegic. His four month stay at [name of hospital] has left us in doubt as to whether he received the care he needed and should have been provided. He was discharged at the end of May with no further instructions, just go home and good-bye.

[Their health insurer] provides an aide for four hours a day, five days a week. [The] county provides an aide for an additional four hours. The only therapy Tom receives is "range of motion" which the aides are instructed to do. A Physical and an Occupational Therapist come to our house once a week. To this day, our son cannot tell us what they do here. A county nurse also comes once a week to take his blood pressure. [Their health insurer] wants to cut out the aide service.

Tom's primary doctor [name], a social worker [name],his nurse [name] and therapists [names] have all agreed that he is getting the best care that can be provided in the home, but that he needs much more. Tom needs extensive therapy which only an in-patient rehabilitation hospital can provide. He needs a hospital that specializes in spinal cord injuries.

Tom has chosen [name of facility and location]. This is a facility that specializes in spinal cord and head injury rehabilitation. Our family doctor has asked [their health insurer] if they would finance his stay. The answer was no, since it's not a local facility. We received the same answer from Medicaid. When dealing with a central nervous system injury, it is unwise to choose a hospital just because it's local. The quality of care has a great deal to do with the quality of life the patient achieves. [Name of facility] emphasizes a balanced, comprehensive and personalized approach to treatment. We want him to regain responsibility for his life. We want him to achieve the highest level of independence possible. This, we believe, is just not possible locally.

Our son's days are spent in one room watching television. He doesn't venture out, because he can't. He cannot feed himself, shave himself, dress himself, brush his teeth or comb his hair. He needs to be taught. If [their health insurer] and Medicaid think by spending thousands of dollars a year for the rest of Tom's life is good for him, then something is very wrong. If they are willing to pay for his rehabilitation, why can't it be where he wants to go for the best care possible? He needs rehabilitation so he can learn to care for himself, to go to school to relearn a trade and to cope with his disabilities so he can become the person he has the right to be. Can you imagine being 23 with hopes and dreams? Your help could make them a reality.

Thank you,
[Tom's parents]

Section II:
Assimilating Persons with Disabilities into Mainstream America

CHAPTER FOUR

Rehabilitation Success: The Relativity of Theory

> *Doublethink* means the power of holding
> two contradictory beliefs in one's mind
> simultaneously, and accepting both of them.
> George Orwell, *1984*

Chris

I met Chris in the fall of 1985 at a day-long conference on computer devices for persons with physical disabilities. During the conference lunch, I was talking with the people at my table about various high-tech assistive devices and noticed, only peripherally, a tray being slid onto the table at the vacant spot to my right. This was accompanied with enough commotion of movement, clicking metal and audible huffs of exertion that my attention was drawn to the distractor.

A tiny woman in her early to mid-fifties, held up by Lofstrand crutches, loomed over me. She had a soft, kind face but one accompanied by an air of truculence.

"Hi, Sweetie. Mind if I sit here? My name is Chris Lofland. I'm OVR's[1] [Office of Vocational Rehabilitation] outback counselor. I say that because my office is in Greene County Hospital. I handle the spinal cord injured cases."

Her voice was strong, a little too loud, and though her words were friendly and warm, they came out crisp, pithy, sharp.

Just a few years before she had left a vocational rehabilitation job in New York City for one here and, in spite of her size and unsteadiness on her feet, retained about her that distinctive air of New York City Tough. As soon as she arrived, she had control over the table and never lost it.

Half-way through lunch she agreed to help me with my research. This bestowal of confidence encouraged another person at the table to do likewise.

We made an appointment to meet the next Friday at her office, the location of which she very precisely detailed to me. Unavoidably, however, I was running late that Friday.

While my mind was focused on meeting with Chris, I still couldn't help thinking, as I did every time I drove towards the parking lot at County Hospital, how very dreary and dismal the century-old place looks. Even after ringing the OVR doorbell at the foot of the ramp to an entirely new entranceway, I couldn't forget the smell of urine, of human deterioration and decomposition that filled my nose even before I left the outdoor air. Sometimes I swear I could take a sniff test long, long after I've left certain places and identify exactly when I was there, with whom, what I was doing and how I felt about it.

I remembered the time I walked through an abandoned ward on the north side of the complex looking for some old videotapes of interviews with patients and their families. The place had been totally empty for five years, but the ward and its furnishings remained as they must have been on the last day of use, as though they wanted to be preserved as a memorial to hospital patients and practitioners otherwise long forgotten.

The beds were set three feet apart and lined both walls of the ward. On them one could easily imagine the people who had lain there over the past 100 years in pain and hopelessness. The stains on the mattresses, the smells that had over many years permeated the furniture and floors, the dismal atmosphere of death were going to hang in that stuffy, sunless, God-forsaken place forever.

The sudden opening of the OVR door startled me no less than Chris' friendly but brusque, "Hi Sweetie, come on in. You're late."

I sensed I shouldn't bother to explain the reasons for my tardiness. Our first exchanges were to bandy about youthful irresponsibility and mature experience. I knew I was getting a lecture frequently given to her clients.

Chris gave me the cook's tour of the OVR suite, originally designed by the Occupational Therapy Department, I knew, as an "apartment" for retraining people to do homemaking tasks. In spite of her hospitality and efforts to make it a homey and cheerful place, nothing could take away the dreariness of a suite of rooms in County Hospital.

We talked for awhile in Chris' office — an average sized room with an old wooden desk piled high with client folders. On the wall were photos of former clients, religious plaques, and Chris' framed certification. After twenty minutes or so, she suggested going into the kitchen area for coffee.

I knew from seeing and talking with her at the conference that she gets around by Lofstrand crutches, an electric scooter and a specially equipped car. But this time, she eased herself up out of her desk chair, armed herself with a pair of wooden crutches and made her way towards the corner by the door to a wheelchair so old-fashioned in design and material that I commented on the use of such antiquities by a rehabilitation counselor in on the cutting-edge of high-tech assistive devices. She said the comfort and ease-of-use of her old devices couldn't be beat and that there's a lot to be said for old tried-and-true friends.

Chris managed her transfer with enough awkwardness for me to offer aid, but she refused and the next thing I knew she was seated and on her way towards the kitchen.

In the kitchen, over coffee, Chris made me feel like an old friend, a colleague and confidante. She told me she had contracted polio just before the age of two and had done most of her growing up in institutions. When speaking of her work there, she mentioned names like Howard Rusk in the same casual manner she would refer to a member of her family.

Her first husband had also had polio. They adopted two daughters and had a happy marriage of twenty years before he died. Chris remarried, and her second husband (able-bodied) is now retired.

Chris had been awarded custody of her granddaughter (for a reason she didn't tell me) and was facing the child's return to her mother — a loss she dreaded. And she had just learned that her office was going to close at County Hospital and be rejoined with the main office downtown.

As for her job, she reported feeling torn many times between the "proper" procedures and doing what she feels would be most helpful for her clients.

> Too much help can be a disincentive to rehabilitation. They're better off if they have to fight some for what they want. But I can't be that hard. When they've shown they can use it, give it to them. Don't be stingy.

She seems to be genuinely concerned for her clients' quality of life, even though her primary focus on the job is their vocational rehabilitation. This she often finds frustrating.

> It often doesn't pay financially for them to go back to work. A good approach would be part-time work because they have to tack on getting-ready time and transportation. Too, their medical needs can be great. But this option is rarely there.

Then she leaned forward and, with a searching tone, added,

Why should we lose these people and these abilities?

Being placed in frequent dilemmas has made Chris somewhat angry with the system, and she attempts to compensate by putting her humanity and genuine caring aside for an objective approach to rehabilitation. She has truly lived five decades of rehabilitation, as a patient and then a professional. Still, she encounters battles such as the most recent one involving a move from County Hospital back downtown.

She spoke not only of her clients but of herself when she told me her perspective of *rehabilitation success.*

> It's not just motivation, it takes a willingness on their part to work. They need to like a challenge... It's like 'I won this little battle,' and it builds you up.

Our coffee klatch over, we returned to her office where Chris proceeded to her file cabinets. Like a bibliophile showing off a prized collection of books, she lovingly touched each case folder as she commented on its thickness (a direct indication of her time and effort spent on the case) and gave a brief life-history of each person whose past and probable future was patiently lying before our very eyes between the file folder covers. She selected a number of likely candidates for my research and then reached for the phone and called each of them to solicit their participation in and cooperation with my project.

Chris's "tough love" philosophy shone through clearly in the phone calls. With one client she was direct and to-the-point as though she were making a business arrangement. With another (Brian in Chapter One) she reassuringly coaxed,

> Brian, your opinions are so very important... you are such a tremendous success, dear.

With one man who had become very obese and withdrawn, she turned to me as the phone was ringing and said, "This one may be tough."

He answered. After a few moments of listening to him she disappointedly but sternly inquired,

> What are you doing to yourself? Killing yourself, that's what! You big lug. C'mon, stop being so lazy. Your biggest problem is *you*, Sweetie.

She did it. Chris got him to participate in my research. After she had hung up the phone she turned to me with a worried look and said, "This guy needs a different approach."

After a few moments of thoughtful silence she added, "That was Butch. Let me know if you get any ideas for helping him, will you."

Always looking for a challenge. But it appears the system is starting to wear her down. Why should we lose these people and these abilities?

Butch, 1986

Even though I had been somewhat forewarned by Chris about Butch's attitude, I was aware while driving to his house that I was feeling quite apprehensive about meeting with him. It didn't help that it was eight o'clock on a dreary, dark March evening.

I drove up to a small Cape Cod-style house in the midst of a congested neighborhood. The house had a still, abandoned air about it even though I could see a couple of lights inside and could hear the faint sound of television. Yet everything seemed so quiet — there were no street noises, no dogs barking — and my knocks on the door sounded loud and aggressive.

After a wait of many minutes and some more knocking, no one came to the door. I got back in the car and deliberated about whether or not I should just leave, then returned to knocking on the door.

This time I heard movement inside and the door was opened by a middle-aged couple who looked at me as apprehensively as I was feeling inside. They were pleasant and polite, but without any delay escorted me upstairs to the long, dark entryway to Butch's annex, pointed me towards his door, and left.

Butch had converted the second floor of the house's detached garage into a large one-room recreation area to be his private domain. It was connected to the second floor of the main house by the long, gently sloped ramp/entryway. After ascending the ramp and coming to his door, I heard a husky, booming growl that set off just about every nerve in my body.

Came in the wrong way, didn't you! I told you to come the back way.

The voice quality was harsh but the tone was one of quite gentle chiding. I opened the door.

Butch's appearance was as grizzly as his voice. A huge man (weighing about 460 pounds), Butch had a brown beard so long and thick that his entire face was covered except for his eyes. And those eyes. The right one was little more than a slit. His total appearance gave him the ability to call forth a foreboding and threatening persona at will. But apparently his overpowering frame and appearance did not provoke a visible reaction in me. Having thus given some impression of strength, I was then presented with a gentle and sensitive man whose very sadness and hopelessness immediately began to shrink his huge and threatening appearance to more ordinary and manageable proportions.

> I'll tell ya'. I had polio when I was 7. My left side was paralyzed. I fought and fought, and I came back from it... I'll be honest, that's one of the disheartening things about this. I fought so hard then, and came back, and now here I'm sittin'. There's no fightin' to come back.

Butch never married, and at the time of his accident lived with his parents as he does now. His gross obesity is due to overeating and no exercise. It is painfully obvious that what was once muscle has become almost pure adipose. He had a heart attack when he was 26 years old, and at 38 it appears he's mercilessly teasing another. He says of his weight problem, however:

> I weighed 200 pounds when I broke my neck... right now I weigh about 460...I just don't do nothin', don't do nothin' physical, nothin' mentally stressing or nothin.' I just sit here and enjoy it. The hell with it, that's the way I see it. No ambition at all, none. Went right down the tubes when I broke my neck. That's the God's honest truth. I'll eat right to the day I die. Have me another heart attack and get it over with. I'm just sittin' around waitin' now. The grim reaper's gonna toll one of these days. Does for everybody, so...

He paused and his affect suddenly mellowed. Then he said,

> I enjoy eatin'. I'll be honest, I have very few things in the world I enjoy doin' and eatin's one of them.

His annex area, made possible by the financial help of no-fault insurance, has a woodburning stove he uses in the winter to keep his place at about 75° to 80°. He needs it this warm because of his poor circulation. Yet, he needs to be cautious as his body temperature regulating mechanism was affected by his spinal cord injury. He has an impaired ability to sweat below his level of injury and needs to protect himself from getting overheated.

His furnishings consist of a complete wet bar, a regulation-sized pool table, a wide-screen television, a short-wave radio ("I know as much as my police buddies do and sometimes before they do") and some chairs and a couch for guests. He spends most of his time now watching television and, when he's feeling particularly inspired, he enjoys writing poetry.

He then offered me "Coke on tap," saying that his place is the only private residence on the regular Coca Cola delivery route. There weren't many decorative furnishings, and a small artificial Christmas tree on the coffee table in March seemed to stand out. Given Christmas should be a rather painful time for him, since he received his injury in December, I wondered why he still had this Christmas tree on display.

Are you just late in putting it away or are you very early for next year?

By this time, I was feeling relaxed enough to try a little chiding myself.

Oh, that's always there. My niece brought it to me in the hospital. Christmas is my favorite holiday.

Four years earlier, Butch was driving home from work in his Corvette one late afternoon when an oncoming car without headlights struck him. His Christmas was spent that year in a state of semi-consciousness. He says he had a premonition that his accident would happen, but that he would be killed.

With a complete injury to his spine at the C7, 8 level, Butch uses a power wheelchair to get around. It has a hydraulic lift that he took great pleasure in demonstrating. By pushing a single button, this huge man grew taller and taller until he towered above me, his head only one foot from the ceiling. He said this option is very useful for getting to those high, tough-to reach places, like top shelves in grocery stores. And didn't I agree that every grocery shopper would find this handy?

Butch has an elevator to take him up and down stairs, one that he and his brother designed and his brother and father built and installed. He only uses it to get to the dining room for meals and to go outside when the weather is good to feed the birds and squirrels that come into his yard.

He also has a fully equipped van that he no longer uses and a Jacuzzi that he can no longer "fit into." This is a lot of expensive equipment to go unused, and I felt compelled to ask,

> Is there anything that would make your van more appealing or useful to you?

Even as I asked the question, I could predict the tone of the response.

> I've lost my ambition to ride in vehicles. I've got about a million and a quarter miles under me and I've been about every place there is to be in this country, part of Mexico, and all over Canada and I've seen just about everything there is to see. Getting in that van and goin' down to the corner store... it just ain't worth that.

Then he talked about assistive devices in general and computers more specifically,

> They're a very poor replacement for what you used to have. And they don't even start to cover what you used to be able to do. And... I ain't no computer whiz. I don't ever want to be a computer whiz. I can't stand them; I hate to even look at the things. And all OVR wants to do now is push the computer.

Butch reported that he perceives himself as having adequate emotional, material, and physical support. He sees few people outside of family, but says he's always been a "loner." As for friends, he offered a rather glib response.

> I've got no friends, got rid of 'em all.
> Why? What do you mean, Butch?
> Friends ain't friends, that's all.

While Butch is paralyzed from the underside of his forearms down, he has full voluntary control of his arms and hands. It was easy for him to grasp our glasses and work the Coke tap to fill them. He is the least severely involved of the spinal cord injured participants in my study. Both Butch and his OVR counselor, Chris, indicated his physical condition and motor functioning capabilities are low. Compared to the other participants with spinal cord injuries in my study, he received Chris' lowest rating on "adaptive behavior" (Brian had received her highest rating).

At the time of his accident, Butch was a driver for a garbage collection service. He says he loved his job.

> There's nowhere I could go and get paid what I was paid and enjoy it, or even do it the way I was doing it, so... You're sittin' here. You know it and you face it. Ain't no gettin' up and walkin' away, so... What can I say? I was used to it in the hospital. I didn't even wanna leave the ward. They had to pry me out of that place... [He choked up a little and then added] I was happy just stayin' there.

In the silence that followed, I thought about his psychological profile which ascribed to him the traits, "nervous," "depressed," "inhibited," "quiet," "hostile," "impulsive," and "indifferent." These data, combined with what I'd been observing and hearing, made me ask about his attitude toward "getting on with life."

> B: I've got a real good *attitude*; it's my *outlook* that stinks.
> S: Well, how do you think you stack up against a 'rehabilitation success?'
> B: I haven't seen one success...I don't know what a success is, as far as sittin' in a chair. I don't know anybody that's a success sittin' in a chair unless they were that way before they broke their neck.
> S: How do you think, then, society defines it?
> B: Keep 'em out of sight, they're out of mind, period. If they don't have to look at ya' they don't have to think about ya.'
>
> [He continued,] As an example, there's this guy where my brother works. He's workin', but he's not a success. He's sittin' there gettin' $2 an hour less than everyone else in the place, the government's subsidizin' his work — and that's being a success? Wrong! No good.

I fished for his definition of the "disabled experience," hoping I'd learn more about what makes him tick than I would from a more direct question.

> B: I wouldn't wish it on my worst enemy. I wouldn't wanna put anybody in this position. There ain't nothin' worse than being stuck. There's nothin' you can do that's gonna change it physically and you know that right off the bat... And when you ain't got nothin' to fight with, then you lose your will. It makes me sick to think about [a $4-an-hour job]. Who

needs it! I sit here with my television set; at least you know who you're talking to.

S: Sounds like you're going to take your 'disabled experience' and hide.

B: That's it. They ain't gonna get a chance at me. I don't wanna be their statistics or nothin.' I'm just sittin' here and enjoyin' it right to the day I die... whenever. Be it tomorrow, be it tonight.

S: Well, then, what would you say about the value of *accepting* a disability?

B: I'll look any son-of-a-bitch in the world straight in the face and say they never 'accept it.' There isn't a single person out there with a spinal cord injury that accepts what happened to them and doesn't wish they could get up and walk away from that chair and set fire to it.

I had asked Brian, too, if he had "accepted" his disability and he had provided a very different response.

You have to accept it, you have to tolerate it. What else can you do? The way I overcome that disability, and the best way I've found, is not to think of it. Put your mind on something else or keep it busy enough where you don't think of it. Some people don't keep their minds occupied. When you think of that one thing all day, that's what's programmed in your mind. But again, that's your personality.

Chris sees Brian as a *rehabilitation success* and Butch as a *rehabilitation failure*. Both men, however, have accommodated themselves to lifestyles they believe to be the most tolerable way for them to live, at least for now. Who can say who's *well-adjusted* and who isn't? Who is and isn't a *rehabilitation success*?

Clearly, many of our cherished rehabilitation concepts are individual constructions.

THE DISABLED EXPERIENCE[2]

Chapter Three discussed the many changes that have occurred in rehabilitation in order to provide an historical perspective of the care and treatment of individuals with disabilities. A more in-depth view of our current time is essential for successfully addressing the needs and concerns of those persons who will live in the 21st century with a disability.

Each person who has spoken in these chapters has described his or her unique *disabled experience* and showed how it is both a personal and a social construction. While it is unique for each individual, it both shapes and is shaped by society's attitudes toward people with physical disabilities in general. *The disabled experience is*, therefore, *an interactive one.*

For Some, A No-Win Situation

Two contrasting views of the disabled experience appeared in a 1983 issue of *Disabled USA*. The first was written by a person with a spinal cord injury who saw rehabilitation as a resocialization process for learning to become a "proper handicapped person:"

> And so, in our defenseless state, without any psychological reserve at the ready, we began our first lessons in learning to be handicapped (Rosen, 1983, p.7).

As Rosen's pre-injury view of "cripples" was one of revulsion, he projected onto society and anticipated the same reaction to himself. Rosen, like Butch, had become handicapped by both society's beliefs about people with disabilities and his own personally and socially constructed perspective.[3]

It is true, however, that as part of a type of resocialization process, a person with a recent disability may be faced with the push to comply with rehabilitation practices that would be vigorously resisted by a non-disabled person. Professional intentions are to offer the best possible help, but they may unintentionally communicate the need for the client to become what Rosen calls a "proper handicapped person." While people are given therapy and training to minimize the importance of their disability in their lives, the concomitant message is given that the disability is so important as to require changes in the most basic elements of their lifestyles.

In Chapter One, Chuck provided an example of how well-intentioned professional objectives can become degrading and demoralizing. He underscored the problem of overgeneralizing a disability in his comment,

> When you're in this condition, people say to you, 'you've got to do it NOW.' They don't look at it like they're looking at themselves, and saying, 'I can put it off until later.' I wasn't that organized before, so why should it change now? I know what has to be done and when it has to be

done and that's what I work on. Your basic style doesn't change just because you're in a wheelchair.

The person with a disability can be placed in a no-win situation or dilemma: To resist therapeutic advice is to risk such unwanted physical consequences as lost neck endurance. To comply, however, may threaten one's self-esteem and need for self-determination.

For Others, the Disability Lost Significance

As a person with cerebral palsy said to me wryly during one of our interviews: Having a disability is a tough job, but someone's got to do it!

In contrast to the angry tone demonstrated by Rosen (1983), Stoll (1983) wrote a companion article emphasizing the role of laughter and humor in achieving a high quality of life. Stoll was born with cerebral palsy and was, therefore, socialized from birth as a person with a disability — her developmental history never included a time as a non-disabled person. The Rosen and Stoll articles taken together highlight not only the individuality of the disabled experience and the variety of perceptions and responses surrounding it, but how this may be variously affected by the person's previous socialization and life experiences.

There can be critical distinctions between the perceptions held by people with acquired disabilities and those born with their disabilities. Individuals who have had whole new worlds opened for them through rehabilitation and rehabilitation technology, such as Jim and Maggie, see the value of assistive technologies differently from those who have had to leave an able-bodied world behind because of an injury as Chuck and Butch did. Individuals with cerebral palsy able to speak for the first time because of synthesized speech output can place a much higher value on that technology than the person who once had, but lost, the ability to speak.

PERCEPTIONS OF *REHABILITATION SUCCESS*

The Independent Living Movement focuses on self-directed choice and advocates the creation of opportunities for individuals to exercise as many free choices as possible. The working definition of rehabilitation used by most professionals is similar in its emphasis on the restoration of a person's physical, sensory, mental, emotional, social, vocational, and recreational capacities so the person can be as autonomous as possible and will be able to pursue an independent non-institutional lifestyle. To achieve this, the rehabilitation professional focuses on functional changes in the individual through physical therapy, education, the provision of assistive devices, and so on while simultaneously considering changes that are possible in the physical and social environment such as the addition of a ramp to a house and the placement of the person into a special training program where there will be peer support. The ultimate outcome is improved well-being — both in terms of individuals' actual physical conditions and the situations in which they live, but most importantly, as perceived by the persons themselves.

It follows that **rehabilitation success** as a professional goal emphasizes the restoration of physical, mental, social and educational and vocational capabilities and opportunities within the shortest possible time. This can mean helping a person *overcome* a disability or *limiting its impact*. Overcoming a disability is the goal of physical medicine; limiting the impact of a disability typically comes under the purview of psychosocial and vocational rehabilitation.

An Ideal Client Doesn't Need Rehabilitation

Definitions of rehabilitation success can seem very idealistic. Kaplan and Questad (1980), in their literature review of "Client Characteristics in Rehabilitation Studies," note that:

> A composite picture of an ideal client can be drawn from the studies reviewed in this paper. The ideal client would be a young, well-educated male with a slight physical disability who would be employed at the time of referral though not making too much money lest he be unmotivated. He would have a good self-concept, high self-esteem, independence, high motivation, specific goals for his rehabilitation, a stable work history and would never have received public assistance. He would have a high degree of acceptance of disability, a high I.Q. and little need for emotional security. In short, the ideal client would probably not need much in the way of rehabilitation services (p. 167).

We are familiar with this view of rehabilitation success because it is the view presented in our newspapers, magazines and on television. It's okay to be *a little bit* disabled. Anything more severe and we are primarily exposed to what people with disabilities call the "super crips;" the "exceptions that prove the rule" that people with disabilities on the average are not as able or capable as non-disabled persons.

Even those articles that try very hard to portray a positive picture of persons with disabilities often end up being written in a patronizing, and thus offensive, style. For example, an article in the December 2, 1990 issue of the *New York Times* featured a college student with severe cerebral palsy and headlined the article as follows: "The Wheelchair Confines Only the Body Inside." The student, who "cruises around campus in a motorized wheelchair and communicates through a computer," has been on the Dean's List each semester since his enrollment and is "a favorite among professors and colleagues who admire his quick wit and sense of irony." One professor called him, "just the average great student" and he is seen as a model of "courage and patience."

As another example, try to pick out the subtle, and not-so-subtle, putdowns in the first paragraph of an article on the Seventh International Summer Special Olympics:

It was hot, the hot kind of hot Indiana hot weather that sends the family dog scrooching under the pickup truck to enjoy the shade. But in South Bend, on the Notre Dame and St. Mary's College campuses, heroic athletes from 70 countries were running and jumping and laughing from the sheer joy of it all. No, these were not the Pan American Games, which were to start a few days later, downstate at Indianapolis. The competitors there, everyone knew, would run faster and jump higher. But not happier; world happiness records were being set here at the Seventh International Summer Olympic Games (Skow, 1987).

The article, "Heroism, Hugs and Laughter," appeared in the August 17, 1987 issue of *Time* magazine. Would this magazine so title an article on the Pan American Games and start out with the same nursery rhyme-style sentences?

A 1991 Harris Poll on Public Attitudes Toward People with Disabilities revealed that people often expressed support of persons with disabilities as a general, abstract concept. When asked about specific situations, such as having a group home established in their neighborhood, they were considerably less accepting. The following excerpt from an article in the *New York Times* shows the public's apparent lack of pathos for an individual with a disability who was innocently injured in an accident:

When a taxi jumped a curb in midtown Manhattan on Monday, two bystanders were struck and seriously injured. Since then, one victim has received four get-well cards. The second has received hundreds of cards; 300 to 400 people have called each day to ask about him, and well-wishers have contributed hundreds of dollars to insure that he receives good care.

The first victim is an elderly blind man. The second is his dog (Bennet, 1992).

Such unconcerned attitudes toward persons with disabilities continue to be one of the major barriers to full and equal societal participation.

Client Motivation is Key

A rehabilitated client is said to exhibit independence and self-reliance while, at the same time, demonstrating a willingness to turn oneself over to and cooperate fully with rehabilitation therapists and other professionals. These apparently contradictory characteristics expected of a "motivated" client can place the person in a no-win situation: Too much or the wrong kind of independence can be perceived as uncooperative; too much or the wrong kind of cooperation can be signs of passivity, depression, dependence.

Nonrehabilitated individuals, on the other hand, have been portrayed as "demonstrating chronic, unmitigated disengagement from themselves, their family, goals, work and society (Starkey, 1967). In addition, nonrehabilitated individuals (like Butch) are described as being angry, resistant to help, and unmotivated. Their depression and hostility provoke rejection from their therapists and counselors, precisely the people who are there to help them. Thus, for the "unmotivated" client, a no-win situation can also exist.

In psychology, there are as many disagreements about the importance of motivation as there are theories to characterize and describe it. For example, Kaplan and Questad (1980) believe that the phrase "a well motivated client" says more about congruence between client and counselor goals than anything intrinsic about the client. Thus, the motivated client is one who likely resembles the therapist in many important ways such as, having similar family income levels and placing the same value on education and work. When people with disabilities have different backgrounds and values, rehabilitation professionals may create "nonrehabilitated individuals" through a *self-fulfilling prophecy*. If professionals believe a person will not succeed in rehabilitation, they may unwittingly withhold resources and assistance so that the individual does become stuck in a cycle of low motivation and poor functional gain. If the person is depressed, passive, and feels he or she is "doomed to fail," the theory of *learned helplessness* suggests low motivation will also result.

Since the traditional medical model has a knowledge flow going in one direction only — from professional to client — individuals who place a premium on their independence, assertiveness, and self-direction may resent and confound attempts to help them. This, too, may result in a state of stuck.

Many Professionals and Clients See "Success" Differently

Many rehabilitation professionals see the "disabled experience" as being fraught with obstacles and attitudinal barriers. Accordingly, they define "rehabilitation success" as coming as close as possible to able-bodied functioning. Rehabilitation professionals emphasize independence, maximization of potential, employment, and societal integration. They tend to judge individuals according to how well they meet this standard of "success."

People with disabilities, however, say that "success" shouldn't require a comparison with able-bodied individuals. It's only meaningful to each individual according to what he or she can and wants to do. *Working* may represent a "success" for one person while *staying at home* may for another. They argue that when a rehabilitation system values only a narrow range of capabilities and goals, an individual's unique competencies and talents tend not to be cultivated.

Ken, a 31-year-old man with a C-6 spinal cord injury from a fall into a ravine behind his house when he was eighteen, has a bachelor's degree in social work and conducts group counseling sessions for an Independent Living Center. His adjustment to his injury was a long and painful process, not made any easier by the death of both parents a few years after his accident. Now both a rehabilitation professional and a person with a disability, he lives independently in an apartment after spending several years in his county's nursing home. About rehabilitation professionals emphasizing able-bodied functioning, he said:

> This is very true. You go into rehabilitation and to them success is going out and getting a job. You can be just as much of a success by functioning

at your highest capability — be it wherever, at work, college or home. There are many rehabilitation successes in sheltered workshops. On the other hand, you can be working in a competitive job and doing a good job, but if you're not working at your full capabilities, then you're not a success. In the public's eye, and in those of many rehabilitation professionals, a rehabilitation success is making $50,000 a year, living in a big house and having three kids. This is the model of rehabilitation held up to us. It does a lot of harm to individuals' self-image and it also encourages society to keep holding this model up. Everyone loses.

Chris and Butch provide just two examples of how different a counselor's perceptions of "success" can be from a client's. Even when a rehabilitation professional and client may seem to agree on the surface, a closer look into their definitions usually reveals the professional's able-bodied bias.

A rehabilitation engineer, for example, defined *rehabilitation success* as follows:

> If through the work we've done we have increased the person's independence or been involved in a situation where it's now a safer and healthier situation (for example, we've provided a seating system that avoids pressure problems) that is what I consider a success.

A man with a spinal cord injury, however, defined *rehabilitation success* more in terms of *psychological comfort* and as being more relative to particular individuals.

> A rehabilitation success is any way you can resume a 'normal' life, no matter if for you a normal life is staying at home. Just as long as you can keep on going with a decent frame of mind. Being successful is just being able to go on living. Being successful is living the way you want to live. You can be successful sometimes and unsuccessful others. It's not an absolute. There's probably as many definitions as the people you're talking to. Part of that is just personality... [and frame of reference].

As noted earlier, even when only comparing the perspectives held by people with similar disabilities, it is clear that two individuals (like Brian and Butch) can have two very different views of "success."

For the most part, however, individuals with physical disabilities agree that the term *rehabilitation success*, like the *disabled experience*, is relative to individual capabilities and experiences. Most see themselves as a success in their own way, and tend to speak in terms of doing what they themselves want to do and as achieving a level of independence that is personally satisfying. They recognize that physical rehabilitation is *not* physical restoration and accept that. They seem aware of the distinction between acceptance of limitations and a focus on negative aspects of the disability and limitations.

Some examples follow of the views of *rehabilitation success* held by people with cerebral palsy or spinal cord injuries. Their definitions are more similar than they are diverse and they highlight many of the same elements: being independent and content — personally satisfied.

> Chuck: Anybody is successful if they are home, and that's where they want to be, and doing okay. As long as they're happy and content with where they are. My idea of success hasn't changed, whether I'm in a wheelchair or not. . . If I decided right now that I didn't want to pursue the computer and wanted to do something else, regardless of what it was, and never left home and was happy, then that would be a success. To me, being unsuccessful is being stuck in a situation you can change and you don't do it, and you're not happy with your present situation.

> Maggie: People with enough faith in themselves.

> DE (CP): Being as independent as your disability allows. Everybody is a success in their own way.

> ST (SCI): Being able to live independently and doing what you want to do as opposed to withdrawing from the world.

> TE (CP): I'm a success because I'm not in an institution. A good mental state is everything. I'm making my own decisions, I got married, I'm living as full a life as I can.

The different perceptions of rehabilitation success held by people with disabilities and professionals may or may not influence the rehabilitation relationship and the resulting services provided. It seems, however, that if rehabilitation therapists or engineers attend primarily to a functional limitation, and do not consider the individual's psychosocial needs and concerns, the person they are striving to help may feel secondary to the disability. Thus, it may just be that the most motivated clients are those involved in a situation where a particular counselor and client rapport has been established and shared perceptions of rehabilitation success exist.

REFERENCE NOTES

[1] OVR stands for "Office of Vocational Rehabilitation." While the name may change from state-to-state, OVR offices throughout the U.S. are federally mandated to help people with disabilities prepare for and retain jobs. This involves arranging for medical, psychological and vocational evaluations and providing guidance and counseling, job training, job seeking skills, work adjustment, and job placement services. Many Independent Living Centers and Client Assistance Programs in the U.S. are funded through OVR state offices.

[2] This phrase is taken from the book, *Ordinary Moments: The Disabled Experience* by Alan J. Brightman (1984, University Park Press). The term, as used by Brightman and intended here, refers to the "every-day experiences associated with [having a disability] as provided by individuals with disabilities in candid and intimate accounts."

[3] Another excellent example of this phenomenon is discussed in Robert A. Scott's book, *The Making of Blind Men: A Study of Adult Socialization* (Transaction Books, 1969). Scott's study reveals ways in which behaviors commonly associated with blindness result more from learned social roles than from anything to do with the loss of sight.

CHAPTER FIVE

Struggles and Strivings

What reinforcement we may gain from hope,
If not, what resolution from despair.
                                    John Milton

Most professionals tend to believe that **rehabilitation success** requires a state of mind, an attitude, that motivates individuals to work hard on their rehabilitation plans. They focus on independence, increased capabilities, and the ability to overcome environmental barriers. As Chris said when asked to comment about this,

> I agree. Rehabilitation professionals definitely see it that way. But the law says that we must have the goal of employment or independent living in the community.

Such a perspective on the part of professionals is, therefore, fostered by a rehabilitation system that emphasizes the achievement of a measurable outcome such as job placement and independence in activities of daily living.

Assistive technologies are seen as valuable enablers of such accomplishments as employment and independent living. Accordingly, when professionals are asked to list the major advantages of assistive technologies, they mention improved functioning, increased capabilities, and enhanced independence.

When rating their clients' functional capacities for this study using the Functional Assessment Inventory (Crewe & Athelstan, 1984),[1] professionals gave perfect adaptive behavior ratings to device users, regardless of disability type. Device users with either spinal cord injuries or cerebral palsy rated themselves on the Personal Capacities Questionnaire as exhibiting more adaptive behaviors than did those not using devices. Thus, all users of devices were seen by both themselves and their counselors as exhibiting more adaptive behavior than non-users.

This focus on the need for individuals to overcome their functional limitations and to adapt themselves to their environments reflects the traditional *individual deficit modification* model of rehabilitation. A high value on assistive technologies is consistent with this perspective and devices are prescribed within this remediation focus. *Environmental deficit modification* focuses on ways to facilitate the integration of people with functional limitations into society and is the intent of such legislation as the Americans with Disabilities Act. Environmental accommodations include ramps into buildings, wheelchair lifts in public buses, elevators, curb cuts, and so on. Individual and environmental deficit modification go hand-in-hand.

Writing for a special issue of *Computer* magazine on "Computing and the Handicapped," an engineer expressed the view that handicapping conditions occur when a mismatch exists between an individual and that person's environment. The mismatch can be corrected in one of two ways: the individual's capabilities can be enhanced or the environment can be modified. He went on to say,

> In a world where human beings and the machines they command have the power to control the quality of life, handicapping can only be the result of failure to properly apply technology or the neglect of its development (Rahimi, 1981).

Two other engineers also see assistive technologies and environmental modifications as being the primary solutions to the functional limitations of a physical disability:

1. There are two models or approaches from which to work: a) modify the world or b) equip the individual.
2. There is nothing wrong with disabled people that the proper environment can't fix... Technology can solve anything... the problem is to get people to use the devices.

Consistent with these statements is the belief that a person's quality of life will be high once "he or she is enabled to walk (or talk, see, hear)" and "once gainfully employed." When coupled with an attitude of confidence in "knowing what is best" for the person with a disability, such assumptions betray a tendency to see assistive technologies as the crucial, and sometimes the only factor needed for successful rehabilitation.

The economic costs of individual and environmental deficit modification may be high, but society's emotional investment is low. So, too, is society's investment in the emotional needs of individuals with disabilities. An unfortunate state of affairs currently exists in which we are making widespread environmental accommodations and are creating more and better technologies that minimize the functional impact of a disability, yet we often fail to provide the more intangible but essential and basic opportunities for assimilation. While accessibility and enhanced functioning are important goals, more crucial are an individual's basic needs for security, autonomy, affiliation, accomplishment, intimacy and identity. As outlined by Norris Hansell in his discussion of people's essential attachments, individuals need to feel connected to the world in which they live — connected to other persons, connected to a social role, to feel that they matter and that their lives are meaningful.

AN ALTERNATIVE PERSPECTIVE

Rehabilitation professionals and engineers strive to minimize individual functional limitations and environmental barriers to the assimilation of persons with disabilities. In contrast, others put forward a *person-centered* perspective. A professional who also has a disability illustrates this difference.

Ken, 1988

Ken is a 31 year-old social worker with a C5-6 level spinal cord injury from a fall. He uses a power wheelchair, modified van, and a variety of low-tech assistive devices. He is so tall that the roof on his van had to be raised to accommodate his height when sitting in his power chair. He wears his brown hair fairly long and has wire-rimmed glasses, reminiscent of the late Beatles star, John Lennon.

In 1988, Ken was a counselor for an Independent Living Center. It is easy to see why he would choose that career. His facial features and expression are gentle and he has a soft-spoken, calm and kind demeanor. His responses are thoughtful, insightful, and sincere. He comes across as someone who could take charge, get the job done, but in a quiet, low-key manner. Everything about Ken says he is truly caring and sincere, but there's also a sadness, a resignation, in his tone that betrays the fact that he became who he is in a rather war-torn way.

As a counselor working for an Independent Living Center, Ken is very active in his community in advocating civil rights for persons with disabilities. His major concern at the time of this interview was increased access to buildings and public transportation. Yet, the first topic he brought up during our interview was a new kind of power wheelchair that can go up and down stairs. He was very intrigued by this wheelchair and hoped that he might be able to have one in the near future. I asked him, "Do you think that's where they should be spending their research dollars, in equipping individuals so that they can go in any building? Or in making buildings accessible regardless of the person's means of mobility?" He responded as follows:

> Ideally, you make the building accessible. If you can do that then each person does not have to have a different adaptation to get into the buildings. Philosophically, if the building is accessible then the person will feel more comfortable going into it — as if they're accepted into the building. If you have to adapt yourself to go into a building, it's like they're saying, 'Well, okay, we really don't want you here, but if you can figure out a way to get in, we'll allow you to come in.'

We continued to talk about the need for improved assistive technologies, access to buildings and the price tag of accessibility. Ken's own words summarizes this discussion well:

> So, instead of going for the real luxuries, as far as going up and down stairs, you first need to cover the basics. It doesn't matter if you can go up and down stairs if you're starving to death because you are alone and you can't get the food to your mouth. First put the money into the necessities of life.

In contrast to the disability-centered viewpoint so often held by rehabilitation professionals, the **person-centered** perspective focuses on psychological and psychosocial changes that enable people with disabilities to manage more effectively in mainstream society. The goal is to create the best personal and environmental climate for individuals with disabilities to achieve their basic needs for security, autonomy, affiliation, accomplishment, intimacy and identity within the larger society.

INDEPENDENT LIVING PROGRAMS: PEOPLE FIRST

Ken is just one of thousands of individuals with disabilities who have adopted an Independent Living (IL) philosophy. The Independent Living Movement was started by a group of consumers who were determined to exercise choice and maximize opportunity and individual autonomy. By 1978, more and more persons with disabilities had moved into mainstream America and the need for institutional care was greatly diminished. The 1978 Amendments to the Rehabilitation Act of 1973 (P.L. 93-112) and the Rehabilitation Comprehensive Services and Developmental Disabilities Amendments of 1978 (P.L. 95-603) provided federal funds to states for the establishment of Independent Living programs. According to Frieden (1980), such programs can be grouped into three basic types:

1. Independent Living Centers - consumer controlled nonresidential facilities providing such services as peer counseling, advocacy, and services around relocation and personal assistance.
2. Independent Living Transitional Programs - educational/training efforts providing individuals with the knowledge and skills to live independently. Training focuses on the development or refinement of skills in the areas of activities of daily living, managing finances, directing and managing personal care attendants, housing selection, and so on. Training may be sponsored by educational or vocational rehabilitation facilities as well as Independent Living Centers and group homes. It may be provided by rehabilitation professionals, educators, consumers, and a combination thereof.
3. Independent Living Residential Programs - consumer-controlled housing where a group of individuals with disabilities determine the services they wish to have provided. Such services often include personal assistance, transportation services, peer counseling, and the development of skills for independent living.

The concept of Independent Living focuses as much on interdependence as it does independence. In addition to peer assistance, persons with disabilities acknowledge the important role of educators and rehabilitation professionals in their attainment of an autonomous lifestyle. A supportive family is crucial — especially when family members are asked to serve as personal assistants.

Assistance is Often the Key to Independence

Assistance from others **can** enhance a person's autonomy. To work or attend school, approximately 20% of persons with disabilities require help in such daily self-care activities as bathing, dressing, and feeding. Family members (parents, siblings, spouse) are the providers of such assistance for over 80% of those persons who require it. According to Nosek (1990), other options for personal assistance include:

a) paid assistants, either full- or part-time

b) assistance arranged through a "barter system" where room and board, for example, are exchanged for assistance,

c) a shared assistant between roommates or another person with a disability who lives in close proximity.

Consumers believe they have more dignity and can exercise more control with full-time paid assistants, but often do not have the funds for such assistance. Thus, there is often a trade-off between low-cost family-provided assistance with the concomitant loss of dignity and control, and other, more costly arrangements which maintain the person's independence.

Nosek (1990, p.3) outlines three levels of need for personal assistance:

a) extensive for persons who could not perform survival functions under any circumstances. [Chuck and Maggie fall into this category].

b) moderate for persons who could perform functions autonomously in emergency situations but require assistance to manage with a reasonable degree of efficiency. [Brian, Butch, and Ken require this level of assistance].

c) minimal for persons who could perform functions autonomously but choose to use assistance to conserve energy and/or time, or to minimize discomfort or damage to weakened muscles. [Jim is an example of a person needing minimal assistance.]

How individuals achieve independence while managing their needs for personal assistance is highly individualized, as the following examples illustrate.

Brian, 1988

In June, 1987, Brian graduated from college and then drove his van coast-to-coast (camping all the way) to live in Berkeley, California. He came home for a short visit the following summer.

Berkeley is great. I definitely have learned a lot since I left. And that was the whole purpose behind leaving; to learn more and to experience more and to live a fuller life. Not that I wasn't living a full life here, but I knew there was more of a life out there. Here, when you're out in the country and there's snow everywhere, you're kind of caught up in your own little space.

It's quite a mind-blowing thing because you have so much freedom, so much independence around there. I mean, there's so many people that are in chairs and so much stimulation because there are so many people around. And there's a lot of people I've met that have been attendants — they've recently jumped into the area and needed some money. They needed a job real fast and this was a way for them to help somebody else and get some money at the same time. It's human relations and a great way to meet people.

Right now my big interest is in recreation. That's where I met Barb [his current girlfriend who accompanied him on this trip home]. It's a great way of getting out in the community and meeting people. Once you get out into the outdoors, it makes... it improves your self-esteem.

I've been out in California a year now and feeling as independent as I can. I've been feeling out my values and looking at what's going to please me, what's going to make me happy in life. I've really taken this year off from work to do that. Now I think I don't want engineering, but something working with people, where I feel I'm benefiting society. Just before I left, my new OVR counselor called and said, 'How'd you like a teaching position?' And I just like, 'Whew, that sounds great.' It would be at a college helping learning disabled students with math. And I love math. It's half-time, so I wouldn't be losing very many of my benefits which is very important when you think about making any sort of big money. Hey, if I got an engineering job, all my benefits would be cut off! I'd rather have a part-time job, keep a lot of my benefits, and have a lot of free time to do things outdoors like kayaking, sailing and rafting. But working and making money is also important and I can satisfy my needs to help by teaching.

When Brian lived at home he relied on his family for his personal care needs. I was curious if he now had a personal assistant.

Through the months I've had a series of roommates. Right now I have a guy from Boulder who helps me with showers, and getting up. I had a girl roommate for three months and she helped me out, too, and we got pretty close. Yet, those things can get too close and, it's like a big slice down the middle. Now that she's gone we've gotten real close again.

I really don't need that much [personal assistance]. And the care that I need, I just ask for it in the morning and at night and the rest of the time I take care of my own apartment and meals.

But I do want that humanistic part. Without people, I wouldn't be where I am now. When I was in the hospital right after my accident, if I didn't have my family and friends coming up and seeing me, encouraging me... I learned off myself talking with other people and it's just evolved. That's why I don't think robotics are the answer for people with disabilities. For example, one of my favorite times was when someone was feeding me. We'd get some good interactions going. You can't do that with a robotic device. It's like... to have your needs met by a robotic device is like saying you're subhuman. But to have someone assist you, to have that conversation, to get to know and live with somebody, it's affirming your value as a human being. It's really important when you can hook up and be just like anybody else and you have human needs that need to be met and the other person can get the same fulfillment out of it. My roommate now gets more out of helping me than I get out of having help. It's giving him a lot of satisfaction. And better understanding.

And so, yeah, it's been a year and I've come back and I've seen everyone. And I said, 'Look, you guys, it's been a year. How have you expanded in a year? This is how I've done it.' I've learned a lot of things. But now it's time to go back there and start a new direction.

Brian illustrates several of the important dilemmas that persons with disabilities face regarding personal assistance. One is the trade-off between a full-time job and the loss of benefits when one's income exceeds the limits set by public sources of support. Another is the management of intimacy and dignity in the face of dependency. The third is achieving a balance between independence and interdependence.

Technologies are being developed to replace the need for expensive, intrusive, often unreliable assistance from other persons. But, as Brian expressed, care cannot be reduced to a technical task. It involves human judgment and understanding. To try to replace more and more interpersonal elements with technical ones can disconnect the individual from contact with caring, supportive persons.

We just do not know all of what is involved when human parts and functions are increasingly replaced by technological substitutes. Zola (1984) indicates it is a mixed blessing. The physiological body rejects transplants and skin grafts it feels are alien to it. So, too, the psychosocial person rejects parts which he or she feels are alien. The more dependent the person feels he or she is on technology for life support and maintenance, the more internally attached and dependent on machines the person becomes, the more the person's identity can become altered.

Jim, 1988

Jim's pride in "walking out of the building with a suit on" has given him the desire to be more like his colleagues at work in all other ways. For someone accustomed to dependency until his early twenties, this has led to a preference to do as much as he can without personal or technical assistance. In 1986, Jim explained:

> I like to have a party once a year for the people I work with. It's amazing how differently they treat me afterwards when they've seen me on my own time. 'My goodness, Jim, you really can do this all by yourself!' They become more relaxed and open. We were just talking a few minutes ago and it's funny, I realized I'm more comfortable around 'normal' people and I think I'm more like 'normal' than handicapped people.
>
> I have a friend with CP, Nancy. After that party I had, she and I went to a CP group and I was uncomfortable and miserable. I'm used to people who do a lot of thinking and talking about work. I couldn't relate to these people because most of them are living at home or working in sheltered workshops.
>
> Nancy reminds me so much of me before my education and rehabilitation. And I was so wrapped up in her... she doesn't want to work, she dropped out of college because they did not let her study what she wanted to and she thought she would pay them back by quitting college. She thinks about her mother dying and she wants to die with her mother because nobody will take care of her. I am more relaxed at work and am more comfortable with normal people. But I was ready to give up work and go with her because I wouldn't have to worry about bills and keeping house. But I got to thinking, 'This is okay, but Monday morning will come and I'm going to work. If I marry her I lose doing things with my friends at work.' I like Nancy, and I think she likes me, but we're often at one another's throat. Even my mother said, 'It'll never work' and I was surprised because she always said, 'Marry a handicapped girl.' I want to be like able-bodied people but I don't think parents have caught up with this yet.
>
> I have too many friends whose parents despise me to death because I'm so outgoing and I don't let my handicap stop me. I'm a threat to their need to martyr themselves.

Many adults with cerebral palsy have led emotionally, socially, and cognitively impoverished lives. They were not given many opportunities for socialization activities, such as talking with others and sharing ideas and experiences, especially if their speech and communication skills were poor. Typically they have not had the opportunity to use these types of interactions to help them establish a firm identity. Often the effect of assistive devices is to thrust them unprepared into a very different world and it can be a tremendous culture shock. Thus, even though trained in accounting, the opportunities presented to Jim until recently prepared him more for a life of dependency than for one as a successful accountant. The more subtle aspects of his career status, such as managing his own finances, were challenging—as he described in 1988:

> The government handouts did good for me. They allowed me to get an education and gave me everything I need but I really did not learn the true value of money until... and am still learning it... when I needed something the money was always there. I didn't understand that it could stop or run out someday. So when I started working I took a cut in money and it took me five years to catch up. Of course, people need the money and the help. But at the same time they need to realize that it isn't always going to be there. And at first, I lived from payday to payday. But I'm learning, and I saved and now I have my own condo. Getting it is definitely not the same as earning it.

Jim's family, always supportive of him, apparently was not prepared for his success and in some respects continues to treat him as irresponsible. Jim very much resents this, as he indicates in the following:

> My family was always supportive of my independence and allowing me to try things out but lately, every time I go back... I get mad at my dad so much! He would rather put down somebody in the family than quarrel or disagree with the person he's really angry with. Now every time we get together with the family he has to get on my case about something, like finances. Then they wonder why I get into a bad mood! I said, 'Dad, can you get a hold of four thousand dollars right now?' And he said, 'No.' 'Then why are you bothering me?' Actually, I couldn't either, but he didn't know that.

Jim's "teenage rebellion" is a healthy one, albeit delayed until his thirties. Some individuals with either congenital or acquired disabilities, particularly those whose family did everything for them, can be dependent, feel powerless and conclude they are unable to overcome their limitations. Such persons may settle into a passive-dependent lifestyle, doing only those things that reinforce their view of themselves as "disabled." Ken articulated this as follows:

> Sometimes you get lost between able-bodied and disabled thinking. I know myself, I side with the able-bodied more. Assistive devices can help improve integration with the able-bodied. If you don't integrate you fall in more with being disabled and may have more of an institutionalized attitude.
>
> People who don't use assistive devices tend to rely on other people and tend to stick with people the same as themselves — who don't use devices either. That's what I mean by an institutionalized mind set. They also tend to believe they don't have control over their quality of life and that community integration is unattainable. For example, alcoholics tend to stay with other alcoholics because they have the same framework. If the people you're with don't keep up with your attitudes, you change to a different group. If you don't want to change groups, then don't change your attitudes.

Jim discussed people who lead passive-dependent, "institutionalized" lifestyles when he talked earlier about his friend Nancy and the members of the CP group he observed:

> I'm used to people who do a lot of thinking and talking about work. I couldn't relate to these people because most of them are living at home or working in sheltered workshops.

Jim's therapist explained from her perspective:

> Institutionalized people had everything done for them — their meals cooked, their beds made — and now fight independence all the way because they lost that critical point where every kid wants to move out of the nest and be on their own. The more severe the disability, the more true this is because people really cannot do many things for themselves. You want people to keep believing they have some control and that something new and exciting can still happen to them. Institutions can sap people of that. Families, too — especially if they martyred themselves and ended up stifling the child and themselves.

Jim, himself, makes the distinction between people with and without disabilities and seems to have internalized the view that those working in sheltered workshops are inferior. Since he aspires to be a "normal person," he avoids others with cerebral palsy saying he is more comfortable around those who are "normal" and share more of his interests. He has yet to grasp, however, many of the more subtle aspects of his career status and desired lifestyle. When corrected or challenged, he feels patronized.

The Desirability of Being Both Person- and Disability-Centered

Those who look beyond an individual's disability and consider capability enhancement within a comprehensive context of attending to individual interests, needs, and background experiences, are being person-centered. They believe it is ultimately more important and cost effective to enhance a person's quality of life, not merely to restore capability. Unlike the *disability-centered* engineer who said,

> In a world where human beings and the machines they command have the power to control the quality of life, handicapping can only be the result of failure to properly apply technology or the neglect of its development (Rahimi, 1981),

person-centered individuals see the environment as presenting challenges, but also stimulation and opportunities for accomplishment. Assistive technologies must pass the acid test of fostering independence and autonomy as well as contributing to a positive identity and to enhanced self-esteem. Being person-centered means looking beyond environmental accommodations and individual functional capabilities to an individual's needs for both independence and interdependence, to the achievement of a higher quality of life.

QUALITY OF LIFE

In 1983, Elizabeth Bouvia made headlines. At age 26, she had lived most of her life "completely disabled by cerebral palsy." With a clear mind but a body in tremendous pain (she also had arthritis), she asked a hospital to permit her to starve herself to death, saying, "You can only fight so long. It's more of a struggle to live than to die."

Elizabeth made the news, not so much because of her desire to end her life, but because of the ethics involved in her efforts to die assisted by the medical profession — an ethical issue very much in the recent news with the publication of a how-to book on "assisted suicide" (Humphrey, 1991) and accounts of Dr. Jack Kevorkian's "Suicide Machine." The sentiments Ms. Bouvia expressed are not uncommon among individuals with severe disabilities who are in constant pain and who feel they have little if any quality of life. For example, Maynard and Muth (1987) reported the case of a man with a severe spinal cord injury who made the decision to end his life. Yet there are many such individuals who, when presented with the means to function relatively independently and achieve valued goals, change their minds and go on to lead long and personally satisfying lives. What may appear to be a bleak existence one day can be changed to a life of contentment and fulfillment — in spite of challenges and obstacles.

Current perspectives and definitions of *quality of life*[2] are fraught with a vagueness which is compounded by the fact that technologists and rehabilitation professionals often have a tendency to make value assumptions about the needs of people with disabilities. As noted in Chapter Four, such assumptions often say much more about professional attitudes and beliefs than anything about the people they are trying to help. For example, data from a study conducted by Evans and colleagues (1985), were used to compare kidney transplant and dialysis patients on their self-reported quality of life. Many of the hemodialysis patients expressed life satisfaction even though they endured under very trying circumstances. To them, dialysis was an opportunity offering life itself. While the quality of life for people with end-stage renal disease may appear bleak by objective measures, the subjective self-reports of the individuals themselves can be quite positive. The authors appropriately note that such incongruity underscores the need to consider quality of life as a highly individualized state that varies over time, and even day-to-day, rather than as a stable trait. A crucial point is, thus, that people can "adapt to very adverse life circumstances, expressing satisfaction with their lives" (Evans et al., p. 58). Similar research findings were reported for persons with spinal cord injuries (Whiteneck et al., 1992).

Just as dialysis machines represent a life line to people with end stage renal disease, individuals with severe cerebral palsy or with a spinal cord injury have found assistive technologies to be important enablers in achieving a high quality of life. Even still, devices have presented their own particular challenges, as the following illustrates.

Ann and Linda, 1986

In 1981, two women with severe cerebral palsy were feeling they had a poor quality of life. Ann, age 42, was ambulatory but with unintelligible speech; Linda, age 52, used a wheelchair and had more intelligible, yet slow, speech. They were both residents of a nursing home where the conditions were "deteriorating badly." It was becoming physically run down and the quality of the care was poor. According to them,

> The attendants couldn't speak English and our speech is not good so there was no communication. Also, we had no privacy. Men, women, anyone would just walk in at any time. They treated us like non-persons and I guess they felt that you can't intrude on a non-person. We were going crazy just trying to stay sane.

Linda had been in that nursing home for thirteen years and Ann for ten. Finally, out of desperation, they thought that together they might be able to live in an apartment, providing they could get daily personal assistance. But that proved to be quite a challenge:

> We couldn't get out of the Home until we got an aide, and we couldn't get an aide because we were in a nursing home.

Eventually, they found personal assistance for four hours, six days a week to bathe and shower them and to cook and clean their apartment. Taking it one day at a time, they tried new things and became more independent. Ann says that, "Since I've been here I've been able to do a lot more on my own."

Ann found that more frequent interactions and communication helped improve her speech; Linda agrees and adds that their ongoing communication helped "sharpen her hearing" so that she understood more of what Ann was saying. Gradually, Ann stopped using her communication board.

> Now I just use it when people don't understand me. Places like the doctor's office where it's important for people to understand me. It's really a last resort. I know myself and when I get anxious I can't talk. I still use it sometimes with Linda to spell out an uncommon word, but it's very slow and Linda's eyes get tired. We've both learned how to relax — my mouth and Linda's ears both have calmed down.

Ann was always more ambulatory than Linda, but found herself using a manual wheelchair more and more. Linda, however, wanted and needed the enhanced control offered by a power chair. This technology presented her with both opportunities for mobility and problems, as she describes:

> I was trying for over three years to get a new wheelchair. It broke down all the time. One day I was going to the store with my attendant and it just stopped in the middle of the sidewalk. They had to go back and borrow Ann's chair for me to use. Three days later I got a loaner. I had to have that accident before I got the new chair. If it wasn't for that, I'd probably still have that old chair.

Ann and Linda were never very eager to venture out by themselves, but that incident with Linda's power chair heightened their concern about getting stranded. When I asked them about using the special vans for wheelchairs provided by their city's public transit authority, they said,

> It's difficult to go out. Transportation is a big problem. They pick you up but to get back home again is unpredictable. We are afraid of going out and getting stranded. Especially in bad weather.

Both Ann and Linda had resolved, however, to conquer their fears and limitations and become even more independent. To them, there were many opportunities just waiting to be discovered. As Linda said,

> Like everyone, we strive for more, for the highest we can get. What is life without striving for more?

When I talked with them in 1988, they had experienced the typical ups and downs in transportation, personal assistance, and assistive technology use, but they seemed to feel more in control of their lives. They had taken a trip to Disney World and Epcot Center and found they could leave their apartment — and even their city — and enjoy traveling and exploring new areas. By 1990, nine years after leaving the nursing home, they had achieved a high quality of life:

Text of Christmas Letter from Ann and Linda, Christmas 1990

> Merry Christmas and Happy New Year to all relatives and friends. Hope this has been a good year for all of you. And the coming year will be even

better.

This has been a pretty good year for us considering everything. The Good Lord continues to bless us with the strength to go on. And for this we are very grateful. We are going on our ninth year in our apartment. Needless to say we are very proud of ourselves.

We did lose our adopted mother and angel Mary, who took care of us for over four years. However once again The Good Lord was with us, as He proved He has more then one angel. We now have Mary's daughter Tracey, who is just wonderful.

This was the first summer since we've been in our apartment that we did not go any place. But you might say we had a vacation right at home. Since we both have electric wheelchairs now, it makes it a lot easier to get around. Up until this summer we were both afraid to cross the street alone. However one Sunday morning Linda said to me "let's cross the street". So I followed. We found out it was not as hard as we thought. After that there was no keeping us home. A lot of our days were spent riding around our beautiful neighborhood. We felt like two birds who could get up and fly whenever we felt like it.

One of the highlights of our summer was a visit from three of Linda's nephews who live in New Mexico. John and Raymond spent a week with us in August. It was so nice to be able to offer them a place to stay. Having them here was like a vacation for us, too. We all spent one day at the Museum of Science and Industry. This was really a treat after not being there for so many years. We walked to the Zoo twice, which is about four blocks from where we live. John found the most accessible way to go with the wheelchairs. So we took about three trips by ourselves after that. Linda even made it alone one day. During our week with John and Raymond we also had a ninetieth birthday party for uncle Fred, who has since then passed away. What a beautiful way to remember him.

During the later part of October Dave surprised us by coming in for a convention. He was able to spend one Sunday evening with us. And came back the next morning for breakfast.

We've had a few visits from our good friend Lois. Even though she moved back to Indiana, she makes [our city] her second home. And does visit us each time she comes in.

Bob continues to be an adopted brother. And is so helpful. Plus taking us to plays, shows, and a lot of places we never dreamed we'd get.

Richard has become a real brother. Quite often he will spend the weekend with us. He will do a lot of things for us. We will either order out, or go out and eat. Then have a lot of fun playing five hundred rummy.

This will tell you a little bit about what's going on with the Rainbow connection. All good wishes for Christmas and the coming year.

Ann

Linda

Ann's and Linda's experiences highlight several problems some people with disabilities have today living independently.

1. Knowledge of and comfort with technology. As women, and in particular women with congenital disabilities, they were not brought up to feel comfortable with and knowledgeable about machines and technical devices. It is evident that only recently have they been able to trust that their wheelchairs will not leave them stranded. Their initial cautiousness kept them from pursuing some opportunities earlier, and others they have yet to pursue. In spite of the opportunities assistive technologies afford them, even making their independence possible, their devices initially presented new challenges. Coming as these challenges did in the midst of other changes in their lives, they no doubt seemed all the more daunting. Yet they received no training in or preparation for their use, and gradually, through trial and error, learned to use them to their benefit.

2. Lack of incentives for older persons' enhanced independence. They were never given the chance to be either "normal" children or "normal" adults. Now chronologically middle aged, but almost childlike in their eagerness to learn and experience what has been until recently unavailable to them, they appear at times to be caught between mature and youthful identities. Older persons with developmental disabilities have special needs that are starting only now to be recognized (e.g. Coelho & Dillon, 1990).

In spite of their consistent efforts to develop and increase their capabilities, their ages make them unattractive to many vocational rehabilitation programs and, thus, the traditional societal rewards for an enhanced level of functioning (job training, education, employment) are not available to them.

3. Difficulties in obtaining personal assistance. Devoid of money, family help, and job skills, not having had experience with such basics as finding a job and a place to live, the odds were against their being successful in living on their own. Through their ingenuity and persistence, however, and with the help of friends and a number of shared personal assistants, they are succeeding. The primary payback for their continued independence — and a very significant one to them — is not having to return to a nursing home. Yet, continuous frustrations in obtaining reliable personal assistance are frequent reminders that many of their gains could be nullified.

Until now, people with severe chronic illnesses or physical disabilities typically did not live far into adulthood. Their continued care past the lifetime of their parents, their primary caretakers, was not a major concern. Now many elderly parents anguish over who will take care of their children after their deaths. And their children are very concerned themselves, as Jim mentioned when talking about his friend Nancy:

> She thinks about her mother dying and she wants to die with her mother because nobody will take care of her.

Maggie, first discussed in Chapter Two, has recently had a considerable functional decline. She and her caretaker moved back to Maggie's hometown to be close to Maggie's mother and other family and friends. Maggie's example illustrates some additional problems aging persons with disabilities often must confront.

Maggie, 1991

I had not heard from Maggie in over a year until one Sunday night I received a phone call from Theresa.

Since Maggie had lost her job with the Independent Living Center in early 1987 ("I didn't learn my responsibilities fast enough — I grew up in a world that didn't teach me how to handle responsibilities — plus I had personality conflicts with my boss"), she had been doing volunteer work helping special education students in a public school. Now, Theresa informed me, Maggie had been in and out of hospitals and rehabilitation facilities for most of the past year. Maggie had surgery on her neck that left her paralyzed from the neck down. As Maggie herself later wrote,

> It started off with loss of function in my left arm and hand, the two most important appendages of my body as I used them for pointing, directing my motorized wheelchair, holding Theresa while she transferred me, and many more things which I took for granted. It ended about eight months later with the loss of function of my legs.

Because of Maggie's changed condition, she and Theresa moved back to Maggie's hometown "to be close to family and friends." The move included Maggie's mother, who had been living in the same apartment complex until "she kept falling" because of back problems. Concern over the welfare of Maggie's mother, as well as the loss of much of her assistance, has enhanced the share of the burden Theresa feels she carries. As Maggie herself puts it,

> Theresa is doing extremely well considering all she has been through with me, especially the move which she was not too happy about. She had spent almost every night with me in the hospitals and had spent every night at Memorial with me, so she just wanted things to be normal again. I, on the other hand, became extremely depressed because the only activity I could engage in was to think of all of what I used to do. There are times now, though, when I think she has accepted my new disability better than I have — or did until the past few months. Before I got my new wheelchair she would say, 'Things will get better when your wheelchair comes' and 'We will just have to struggle through it like I said before your surgery.'

Maggie now needs new assistive technologies because her condition has changed so much. Both Maggie and Theresa needed to get used to these changes, which added more stress to what each was already feeling.

> After my neurologist ordered a MRI, it turns out I have what is called a swan neck deformity. When I put my head forward my spine closes and the fluid stops flowing. When I put it up, the fluid starts again. I came home with a cervical collar and a corset, more for support than for correcting the problem as the doctors assured me I couldn't get any worse.
>
> Everyone was holding their breath when my motorized, reclining wheelchair arrived as I could still sit up when the seat and back were made and the chair was ordered. To everyone's relief, the doctor said I didn't need either the cervical collar or my corset when I used the wheelchair. I was especially glad, as I didn't like to look that disabled, or you could say, I wasn't accustomed to having that many people stare at me. Even though I've had a disability life, little did I know that the new chair would really cause people to stare — but more out of amazement than pity. The chair itself is the optimum in high-tech. It is all controlled by using a joystick which I hold in my mouth. This enables me to be in the recliner mode, the drive mode, and the Light Talker mode, meaning

I can use my communication device in this mode. I change modes by pushing a button at the side of my head. People have said it looks like a rocket, especially when I'm tilted all the way back.

Luckily, there was a one-time grant given through the state and people from UCP suggested I apply. It and Medicaid paid for the wheelchair. It paid less than one fourth of the cost of the Light Talker. Fortunately, I bought the van before all this happened or there would have been the additional expense of purchasing one and having it customized. Without it, I would be stuck at home as it is impossible to get my chair in a car. Mother helped pay for the Light Talker which gives me a means of communication.

UCP has a program to teach people how to use an IBM computer and then finds employment for them. I am going to enter it in early '92 as, if I can, I would like to have a part-time job writing or doing something along those lines. Anyway, it will do me good to learn more about IBMs and to know that I may be able to become productive again.

Maggie's experience illustrates some additional challenges in helping aging persons with physical disabilities maintain their quality of life:

4. Added stress on already burdened caretakers. Family members and other caretakers who devote a major portion of their day to the care of their loved one with a disability may feel overwhelmed by the heightened need for medical and technological interventions. When, in spite of such assistance, they see the individual continue to deteriorate or become depressed, they may experience their own sense of helplessness and despair.

5. New device and equipment needs. Aging persons with disabilities undergo changes in their physical capabilities and general health that require modifications in devices and heightened attention to their special needs (e.g. Holland & Falvo, 1990). Maggie illustrates this, and so does Chuck. In 1991, Chuck had been in intensive care after a severe case of bronchitis.

My carbon dioxide level was high and now I need to be on oxygen all the time.

Yet, he tries to get out as much as possible and

When I'm out shopping or go out to eat I don't use the oxygen.

Rehabilitation engineering efforts will also need to address functional declines and the preservation of as much previous functioning as possible.

There is a dynamic interactive relationship among assistive device use, quality of life, functional capabilities and temperament, and this relationship can change over time. Therefore, this constellation of factors needs to be continually addressed, first from a person-centered perspective, and secondarily from a disability-centered one.

Another key for appreciating how — and why — some people with disabilities attain a high quality of life while others do not, is understanding the various ways individuals strive to satisfy needs and establish an identity in today's society. It is to these topics we turn in Chapter Six.

REFERENCE NOTES

[1]   The Functional Assessment Inventory (FAI) is a 30-item measure of six functional areas: Adaptive behavior, vocational qualifications, communication, motor functioning, physical condition, and cognitive functioning with two additional items assessing visual impairment and the need for special job requirements. There are also ten special "strength" items and two Likert-scales for rating disability severity and employability. Respondents are typically rehabilitation counselors or other vocational rehabilitation professionals. The FAI manual (Crewe & Athelstan, 1984) reports inter-rater reliability and both concurrent and predictive validity of total FAI scores. A companion instrument, the Personal Capacities Questionnaire (PCQ), is an item-by-item translation of the FAI into statements completed by a consumer regarding him or herself. Field testing of the companion PCQ is currently underway. Both the FAI and PCQ require respondents to evaluate each of the 30 items on a four-point ordinal scale that ranges from "no significant impairment" (score = 0) to three levels of increasing impairment to a maximum score of 3.

[2]   In the realm of bioethics, the consideration of quality of life has most commonly centered on such questions as abortion and euthanasia (Reich, 1978). Advances in biomedical technologies have also raised questions about the relationship between depersonalized care, patient isolation and alienation, and quality of life (Mitcham & Grote 1978).

Sociologists typically use the term "quality of life" and rely on a variety of social indicators (such as health status, crime rates and economic trends) to characterize it (Blau, 1977; Szalai & Andrews, 1980). While there is no single definition of quality of life, most authors on this subject agree on two points:

a) "The best approach is probably to accept 'quality of life' as a single indivisible generic term and to attribute at first some vaguely circumscribed meaning to it that can be subsequently clarified and specified by more research and reflection" (Szalai & Andrews, 1980, p.9).

b) It is best assessed through a combination of objective and subjective measures.

Most recently, *quality of life* has been described as life satisfaction, well-being and general affect. It has been studied by looking at subjective reports along with such objective indicators as socio-demographic and medical factors, functional impairment, and ability to work (Anderson, 1982; Campbell, 1976; Chubon, 1985; Evans, Manninen, Garrison, Hart, Blagg, Gutman, Hull, & Lowrie, 1985; Fabian, 1991; Katz, 1987; Scheer, 1980).

Alexander & Willems (1981) advocated behavioral measurements of person-environment interrelationships and interactions to assess quality of life; Kottke (1982) similarly emphasized a person-environment fit for life quality; and Flanagan (1982) applied his critical incident technique to survey data obtained from a general sample of 1,000 people (in three age groups) and extracted 15 quality of life components. Roessler (1990), addressing rehabilitation specifically, presented a comprehensive interactive model of quality of life.

CHAPTER SIX

Myths and Machines

"There is some Myth for every man, which if we but knew it,
would make us understand all he did and thought."
William Butler Yeats

As we continue to be so fascinated with the potential benefits of assistive devices for persons with disabilities, we often fail to fully consider the quality of life of the individuals who will use these technologies. *Quality of life* considerations require focused attention to a person's achievement of higher level psychological, social and cognitive functioning in spite of limitations in physical functioning. All too often, however, the emphasis is on the physical aspects—improving *quality of life* through the use of assistive devices to the near exclusion of other needs, such as the user's social and emotional needs.

Carolyn Vash, a psychologist who has quadriplegia, has presented a typology of *determiners of disability* (1981) that reflects the range of factors one must attend to:

1. Physiological Factors—Physical Condition of the Self: The nature of the residual disabling conditions as determining the "disabled experience". Varying states of health can lead to different complications and sequelae, courses of treatment and rehabilitation. Beyond individual physical characteristics, functioning also depends on such factors as the person's environment(s), resources, e.g., private insurance for specialized treatment, and opportunities, e.g., placement in a rehabilitation center equipped with the most advanced rehabilitation technologies.

2. Psychosocial Factors—The Attitudes and Responses of Others: The environment as social determiner of the "disabled experience". The attitudes and responses of others, expressed by the interactions within the family or through exposure to the responses of others can have a profound influence on the person with a disability. Self concept, motivation, and personal aspirations of an individual may be shaped by social interactions that influence positive personal regard, resources and opportunities.

To illustrate: there is a strong deaf culture found at the National Technical Institute for the Deaf in Rochester, New York. The student peer groups greatly influence individual student decisions regarding the types of communication technologies they will use, such as one's mode of hearing amplification. A person's social support network can greatly affect the *disabled experience* and may even influence daily functioning and rehabilitation outcomes. Social support systems have a profound influence on how people with disabilities interpret their experiences, evaluate their options, and may even affect what alternatives the person with a disability may view as available initially. Further, the ways in which rehabilitation professionals define the *disabled experience* and *rehabilitation success* are potent environmental influences on individuals with disabilites.

3. Psychological Factors—the Attitudes of and Toward the Self: Individual Differences as Determiners of the "Disabled Experience." People with disabilities, even the same disability, have different perspectives about their limitations and capabilities. They vary in their views of what living with a disability is like and their course of adjustment to the disability. Their temperaments and ways of coping with the persons and situations in their life space are factors influencing such differences.

Theories of personality can help the rehabilitation professional understand the roots of depression, anxiety, anger, substance abuse, loneliness, social isolation and other phenomena often encountered when working with persons who have cerebral palsy or a spinal cord injury. An explanation follows regarding how different clients come to define their "disabled expeirence" as they progress though a course of recovery of function.

Towards self-actualization. Abraham Maslow (1954) theorized that persons developed along a hierarchy of five levels of needs and ranked them in the order in which individuals satisfied them:

1. Physical
    a. survival
    b. security
2. Social/affiliation
    a. belonging

   b.   esteem
3.   Intellectual/achievement
   a.   knowledge
   b.   understanding
4.   Aesthetic
5.   Self-actualization[1]

Maslow maintained that needs must be met at each successive level, beginning with the most basic, *physical needs*, before one moves on to the next. Frustrated needs result in hostility and/or anxiety. Maslow's theory illustrates common attributes of a developmental theory. Persons cope successfully with ever more complex behaviors as they live and grow in a widening range of areas, building on successful earlier achievements and moving to more complexity. It is easy to see this range when one compares the complexity of behaviors evident among adults as contrasted with children. When a young adult who had functioned at the higher levels receives a traumatic injury (such as a spinal cord injury) he or she has to re-focus again on the satisfaction of more basic physical needs. Often such adults find themselves having to go through each successive stage again, meeting the needs for affiliation with new friends and achievement needs in an entirely new career area than originally planned.

   In a parallel fashion, when a person grows up with cerebral palsy and his adjustment to this condition is sharply altered by assistive devices so that he can perform tasks he could never do, the person's desire and drive to continue to progress through higher levels of the hierarchy pose difficulties he could never have imagined prior to his improved capabilities.

   In the next sections, these situations are examined from the perspectives of persons who have attained high levels of functioning, but want and yearn for more—in the vernacular of the 80's—they want it all!

Jim, 1988 continued

Earlier we noted that Jim was becoming a "reluctant user" of assistive devices in favor of no longer needing them and being able to do things without them. In 1988, he said,

> I've been walking around a lot lately and I'm getting run down and worn out physically.

The physical toll on him is one thing, the emotional another. The man I was talking with in 1988 had become quite different from the one I had met two years before.

> I met a woman who works in a bar I was hanging out in. Since I walked in, she only saw me sitting there at the table like anyone else. She didn't know I use a wheelchair. So without knowing that, she invited me out for a drink. But then when she saw me get my wheelchair, she made some excuse for not being able to go out, for being tired. It just blew her mind.

He had related several anecdotes that had involved him in bars. I was becoming concerned that Jim might be developing a dependence on alcohol. I didn't want to sound confrontive, so I adopted a more indirect approach.

"Even though you can do everything at work that your colleagues do, it still sometimes takes twice or three times as long, so that frustration and physical exhaustion can set in. A lot of people in that situation either drink too much or use drugs. I was wondering if you would know why and what can be done about that?"

> I think I drink too much. It helps me to unwind and maybe to deal with my frustrations. It's probably a little bit of both. I drink a lot more during the week but I think the only regret I have, in order for me to relax, is companionship. I feel I'm normal in every way but in companionship. I think it's the emptiness.
>
> It's not the lack of opportunity, it's the lack of confidence. In my family, we just don't talk that much. I never learned how to express myself and to be less passive.
>
> My friend says I live in a dream world and he is making me aware of how I try to make a fairy tale life out of a relationship and I've got to stop doing that so I don't get hurt.

Jim now finds himself caught in several dilemmas: Thanks to the rehabilitation services he received, he was trained for a job that he likes and has succeeded in. His co-workers treat him as both a colleague and friend and try to help and further socialize him. He is trying very hard to form an identity as a "normal person" and he finds it difficult to tolerate the company of other people with disabilities similar to his own.

Yet, Jim's vocational success has led to his desire for equality on other dimensions for which his prior socialization did not prepare him. Jim's continual striving, identity confusion, and physical exhaustion have taken an emotional toll on him to the point where he seems to be frustrated, insecure, and depressed — which he largely attributes to the attitudes and faults of others.

Jim's confused identity has also led him to make some rather poor judgments. He did not use his assistive devices. As a result he became physically "run down." He interpreted the motives and actions of others in a defensive manner; for example, his difficulties in identifying with other people with disabilities was due to their shortcomings ("I get interesting vibes from other handicapped people. They are embarrassed for my success because it makes them look lazy"). As seen in Chapter Four, when his father inquired into his financial health, it was not because of Jim's inability to handle money, but because of his father's inability to appropriately handle anger and/or guilt. The following statement shows that Jim also ascribes to his father feelings which the father has projected onto his other children.

> My dad wants to repay my brothers and sisters for the shame they endured because of me when we were younger and they were ashamed to have their friends over. But they themselves say they've never felt ashamed.

When asked about Jim's "identity-crisis," his speech therapist provided the following:

> Compared to persons in sheltered work situations, Jim gets along beautifully. But when he's out in the community, people are not comparing him to people in sheltered workshops, they're comparing him to his non-disabled colleagues.
>
> Often, by increasing individuals' functioning to an almost able-bodied level, it may occur that these same individuals can't deal with the frustrations they've suddenly been faced with. Many people have very unrealistic expectations. We see it in parents, employers, vocational rehabilitation counselors, speech therapists, the physicians here. Many people think that once that person has the appropriate technology, that the problem is going to be solved and that person is going to be 'normal.' It's just not true.

And another rehabilitation professional concurs:

Someone who is very high functioning cognitively is very aware of what the rest of the world out there is like. They have an 'I am really different' perspective. They may look at others and say, 'Boy, wouldn't it be great to be that way.' They may have had a fantasy of wishing to be like everyone else. When they see a good deal of progress towards normalcy, they tend to overexpect things to happen as a result. Employers, everyone, now are expecting more, as well. But often it's a whole new world of frustrations that opens. Mobility may no longer be a frustration, but relationships are.

We all cope with frustrations in our lives according to how we've coped in the past. People with CP have had much more limited experiences to garner [good] coping strategies and with such dramatic changes now available to them — probably more than the average person will ever experience — plus real physical limitations, the emotional experiences and anxieties can be tough.

The optimism around the elimination of *individual deficits* has led to higher expectations on the part of some families, professionals and employers. Perhaps no higher expectations exist than those individuals with disabilities often have for themselves. Jim's example continues to be illustrative:

Jim, 1991

The first thing Jim said to me when I called to tell him I was going to be in his city for a conference was, "Guess, what? My picture is being shown all over the world."

We had agreed to meet one late afternoon in the lobby of the conference center. Then he suggested we go to a bar saying, "In this city after work, you can get a free dinner from the snacks served in the bars."

Jim was dressed in a navy blue striped shirt, red tie, and light blue suit. His tie was worn loose, like other men in the bar who had just left work.

As soon as we were seated he showed me the cover of his company's annual report. There he was, front and center, and around him were a couple of older workers and members of a variety of ethnic groups. Again, he talked about his international exposure.

Then Jim brought me up-to-date on his family. His father died in January, 1990 of cancer — he was sick for close to two years. In that time, Jim drove to visit him almost every weekend. At the same time, he was in a car pool and would take other people to work. "All told, I put about 50,000 miles on my van in one year."

Jim had to sell his condo because he fell two months behind on his payments which he attributed to traveling so often to be with his father. They told him he either had to pay the entire remaining balance or give up the condo. He had to do the latter and now lives in an apartment downtown.

Jim is so financially strapped that he is also in the process of selling his van — his second. Now that he lives downtown, he can get to work on his scooter and he says he only needs to drive his van about once a week. When he gets the money from the sale of his van, he wants to go to Las Vegas.

Then he talked about how things were going at work. He was disappointed with his most recent raise, and said that people have told him that he's not paid well. I asked about the prospects for a promotion, and he said, "Not in the near future. If someone offered me a better paying job, I'd take it." I had the impression that he felt his company should pay him more in exchange for the privilege of being able to feature an employee in a wheelchair on the cover of their annual report. I then asked him about returning to school to finish his degree. Jim answered, "It's hard after working all day with computers and ledger sheets and books to do more with that."

He said he leads an active social life and added that his interest in being around people with disabilities is just about gone now. Then Jim told me that, "Ten weeks and one day ago my heart was broken" by a woman who was a cocktail waitress and model. They had been going out for about six months. He talked about the movies they had seen and that he had taken her out for dinner on numerous occasions. Then she suddenly told him that she no longer wanted to see him.

The last couple of months, he says, have been very rough on him. He wants a romantic relationship but feels very discouraged about having one soon. He said that people with disabilities are not seen as desirable sexual partners and gave an example of going to a "strip-tease place, one I often visit, where the dancers do a routine with the men but they wouldn't with me."[2]

We had been talking for over an hour when Jim suddenly announced that he had forgotten something at work that he needed to have that evening. He finished his drink and, without having any of the snacks they served, paid the bill. As we were making our way back out, he told me that he is very glad he was able to be with his father when he died, and to be with him through his long illness. But he's sad that his father died not knowing how capable he is. And his mother is still in the process of becoming aware of his capabilities. Then he said that one of his sisters has a habit of "popping in" on him and cleaning his apartment and bringing him groceries. While he loves his sister, it was clear that he interpreted her caretaking as "patronizing" and, once again, said that, "My family just doesn't trust my capabilities."

Beyond Companionship to Sexual Expression

Having a job has turned out to be an incomplete victory for Jim. He now is striving to attain the skills, confidence and ability to cope with all of life's opportunities and challenges, and the chance to fall in love — to develop an intimate relationship. He had said in 1986,

> Recently, though, I've started to think... I've been too busy with my independence to go out and relax, to date. So now I'm alone. I feel it is time to have [an intimate] relationship. I realized I wasn't going to do it where I work because if you go the handicapped route you're not exposed to too many handicapped people there, and when you are, it doesn't work out the way it's supposed to. But with AB's [able-bodied persons] I can't go so fast. [With one girl in particular:] It's hard for me to get out my feelings...I've been too busy with my handicap to know what that's all about.
>
> [Later he added,] I'm struggling and striving for what? To live alone? There's a beautiful girl out there... Every time I give up something positive happens. Like when I gave up on trying to drive. And I gave up on a job.

Jim's confusion about wanting a relationship with another "handicapped" person or with an "able-bodied" woman is not unusual. A similar dilemma was heard from Ken:

> As far as living with somebody or getting married, I could never marry, I don't think, a...nother disabled person or somebody in a wheelchair. Friendship-wise, it's split about half-half. But as far as a relationship, I just can't picture being with somebody I depend so much on. It would just be too many hassles. It'd be cumbersome physically, and emotionally also. I think a lot of times, too, there's a trade-off. She helps out more in the physical part, I help out more on the emotional part. [With another

person with a disability] there'd be no trading-off, it wouldn't be complementary. But as far as identifying, sometimes both, sometimes in-between and sometimes neither.

Most of the individuals with physical disabilities in this study said they were very lonely; that they desired physical contact and intimacy, to have their bodies be accepted in a romantic or sexual way. For example, Chuck talked about wanting to meet women but believed that they have "a tendency to move away from me... It's hard to approach somebody when you're in a wheelchair, as opposed to the way it was before." Brian, too, expressed the wish for a girlfriend: "it would be all that much... more." Maggie wishes she had "more of a social life."

In an article titled, "Not a Fifth Wheel: Sexual Expression Needs to be Mainstreamed, Too," William Rush (1985), a 28 year-old journalist with cerebral palsy, believes that his "struggle for self-sufficiency has been so significant that a relationship at this time is out of the question." He echoed the sentiments of Jim, Ken, Chuck, and Brian and goes on to say how hard it is to get to know people, especially if you're shy; that power wheelchairs prevent people with disabilities from getting close to anyone.

> And when I'm bent over my letterboard or voice synthesizer, spelling thoughts out with my headstick, I can't establish eye contact.

His cerebral palsy is the type that results in uncontrollable muscle spasms:

> I can't put my arms around a woman without the risk of giving her a black eye.

While he realizes his body "is far from perfect," he notes that society does not perceive adults with cerebral palsy as interested participants or as desirable partners because they're viewed more as "eternal children" than as sexual beings and potential love partners. People with cerebral palsy, have masculine and feminine identities which influence their relations in general, and he states that intimate relationships are needed

> because we would be incomplete and unable to live totally alone. We need companionship and to care about others and to be cared for and about.

With a determined, and somewhat angry tone, he adds,

> My problem is not faulty equipment... I know I'm capable of loving and
> being loved. And I'm tired of being told I can be independent while being
> denied the chance of being interdependent; I'm tired of being told I have
> so much to offer society while being denied the opportunity of giving my
> love to another person.

Emotions Run Deep, But Lie Hidden

The subject of sexuality for people with disabilities has generally been
taboo. Until fairly recently, many people born with congenital disabilities like cerebral palsy were subjected to surgical sterilization. In fact,
people with disabilities have been given the strong message to hold in
check most of their feelings, especially anger, frustration, and sadness.
For today's adults with cerebral palsy who were often isolated and
dependent on their parents as children, a habitual demeanor of being
docile and complacent has been a frequent result.

Most people with disabilities are implicitly or explicitly encouraged
to avoid the negative emotional sides of their lives. This may be especially
true for those in spinal cord injury rehabilitation centers. The young man
injured in an automobile or motorcycle accident, or by a gunshot wound
or a sports injury, likely has a great deal of anger over the injury, its cause,
and its often unavoidable consequences. To allow the expression of
strong anger is to risk violent outbursts. Unvented anger, however, can
manifest itself as depression, illness and/or resistance to rehabilitation.
A typical course of action is to glorify courage and toughness by idealiz-
ing others who exhibit these characteristics.

Ken, 1988 Continued

Fifteen years after his injury, Ken shared his perspective on the emotional
aspects of rehabilitation. The book, *Options* (published by the National
Spinal Cord Injury Association), that he mentions is one that was
circulated on his spinal cord injury floor in 1974. It contains case examples of people's lives after their injuries and is meant to be inspiring.

> What's needed is a good middle ground between the attitude expressed
> in the book, *Options*, where you feel like a failure because you know

you'll never match up to the guys in that book — who all have a $200,000 a year job, a wife and kids, a big house and brand new sports car — and the need to have some hope held out to you, which *Options* does to an extreme and which can destroy a lot of people attitudinally. Initially in rehabilitation you need a ray of hope. It gives you something to work toward. But professionals should be more realistic by telling people that, 'This is possible, but not likely for everyone.' As rehab moves along, they should emphasize more and more each person's own capabilities and what is realistic for that person. They also need to get people to see that their disability doesn't need to stand in the way of their achievement. You're going to have failures, but you're also going to have successes. Without trying, you're not going to have either.

I wasn't assertive before my injury and that helped because the more aggressive guys [with a lot of hostility and intolerance] have a tougher time with their injuries.

Some people just need more time than others. There were people up on the floor that hated going to therapy. There was no motivation there whatsoever. So, for them, maybe therapy wasn't the answer at that point. They were the ones that got left by the wayside. The people that would come into their sessions and do what was expected, the staff seemed to concentrate more on them.

Some rehab professionals try to make silk purses out of sows' ears, and that isn't being realistic either. Rehab needs to have the attitude of, 'Okay, this is what you have, and this is what you can work with. What can you do to make the best out of what you can work with?' They need to focus mainly on those people that are going day-to-day through life, just like the average able-bodied person goes day-to-day through life.

Ken's perspective was formed after a slow recovery from depression and prolonged rehabilitation, which he likened to Elisabeth Kubler-Ross' stages of dying (1969).

If someone is stuck in the grieving process... six to seven years is the average for real adjustment. It's like an adjustment to a death. The only thing is, for an injury or disability, it's not as easy to adjust as with a death because with a death, the person's no longer there. With a disability, you have a constant reminder. So, sometimes it takes even longer to grieve and adjust. A lot of people turn to alcohol and drugs, which is a way of going through denial. As long as you're smashed or stoned, you can forget about your disability. It alters the mind and you can forget about it. Well, you don't forget about it — you just don't quite care as much.

I asked Ken for his opinion about how common it is for people with spinal cord injuries to use drugs and alcohol to avoid confronting the facts of their disabilities. He continued,

> Everybody goes through that stage, I think, of using a lot of alcohol or drugs. It's just a coping mechanism. Some break out of it and some don't. I know people who've stayed smashed their whole lives. If you use it just for a while, it's a good coping mechanism. You're usually left alone by society because when they see somebody with a disability, and see they're an alcoholic, they say, 'Well, they've got enough problems. Let them be.' Even rehab, we used to be able to drink all we wanted. The hospital even supplied it. Just as long as you'd do rehab the next day, it was okay. I don't know exactly why. I think maybe because the doctors knew that no matter what they did for us, it was still inadequate. But now that policy has changed because they had too many problems with people getting really smashed and getting into fights. And one nurse's aide on drugs snapped out. I believe you can still get a couple of beers, but not as much as you used to be able to get.

Rohe and DePompolo (1985) reported the results of a survey of rehabilitation unit personnel on their substance abuse policies which indicate both that substance abuse is quite prevalent and that the policies on Ken's rehabilitation unit were not uncommon, nor Ken's hunches inaccurate (see also Heinemann (1991), Benshoff, Janikowski, Taricone & Brenner (1990), Greer (1986). Ken summarized his perspective of adjustment for the person with a spinal cord injury as follows:

> A lot of it is just time. Rehab can't turn your life around in just a couple of months.

Many people with disabilities need time to develop an awareness of their disability and a perspective of themselves which allows them to admit grief and anger and then get on with their lives. Some need months; others need years. For Ken, it took a major life event to turn himself around.

> It was a slow process getting fed up with doing nothing. It was like a long, low-grade depression I didn't even know I had until I came out of it. It was just, I was unmotivated. I knew it even while I was doing it. But even when I was in the stage of depression or whatever, in the rut stage,

I saw both the positive and negative sides. I never had a real negative attitude. I was in the stoned part, but I wasn't negative. I always tried to keep an optimistic attitude. I think that's what helped me to get out of the depression and progress through the stages.

One of the things that did it, also, was not something I was glad happened and that was my mother's death. My mother, and all my family, were very over-protective — but especially my mother. After she was gone, there was not so much of a dominant figure, so then I had to kind of learn to find my own way. My father... he was a very passive person, a farmer most of his life. He died two years ago and he kind of took things as they came and just went through life. Good or bad, I modeled him in a lot of ways... Even though I went through the depression and stuff, there's not a lot of ways to change things. You change things when you can, but you don't go out and constantly knock your head against a wall to try to beat down the system and this type of thing. You make little changes where you can in a... quieter way. And it does work. Once you can achieve smaller goals, you can work up.

Through my years I've seen both sides of it. I mean, I've been in rehab so many times they don't want to see me again! But I've seen everything from really high achievers to suicides, you know, people that are planning suicide. Or a couple of people that I know of that are drinking themselves to death. It's just that different people look at it in somewhat different ways.

WAYS OF COPING CAN AND DO DIFFER

As with *rehabilitation success* and the *disabled experience*, adjustment is dynamic, situational, and often "in the eye of the beholder." People vary as much in *how* they adjust to and cope with physical injury and permanent disability as the extent to which they *do* adjust and cope. One may cope well at work, but not with the situation at home; a while later, the situation improves at home but then new challenges develop at work which are very stressful. Too, a person may feel that he or she is coping well only to be told otherwise by rehabilitation professionals, employers, or family members.

As it is true for people in general, some individuals with disabilities cope with their challenges earlier and better than others. Some pursue a productive and satisfying life, others are "just sittin'" for a time, and still others seem destined to have their efforts to achieve a particular lifestyle repeatedly frustrated.

Brian said in 1986, "If I come across something that needs to be done, or that hinders me in any way, then I'll find a way that'll work." Butch, on the other hand, tended to give in to the obstacles posed by his spinal cord injury, "... now here I'm sittin.' Now there's no fightin' to come back." Some individuals with spinal cord injuries will harbor hopes for a cure and not develop career or lifestyle plans compatible with their present capabilities. Some (like Ken and Brian) share an unwillingness to be held back from pursuing their independence and goals. Others seem to lack motivation for increasing their independence.

Several participants in this research reported having confused identities and feelings of being alienated from the rehabilitation system and from their peers who either do or do not have disabilities. At various times they reported nervousness, depression and inhibition which suggests that the identities of these persons with disabilities are somewhat fragile. While many emphasize goals they have, their desire to work around obstacles and the value of their assistive technologies; others focus on obstacles as being insurmountable. Some presented themselves as meeting challenge head-on; others as feeling defeated.

All individuals who completed the Taylor-Johnson Temperament Analysis in 1986, 1988, and 1992, showed variability over time which was reflective of changes both in their adjustment and circumstances. For example, over the three administrations Butch moved closer to a more well-adjusted pattern; Maggie's profiles reflected her grief over her father's death and her vocational insecurities. Such results are not definitive, yet they demonstrate that people with disabilities adjust in various ways over time, that there is developmental growth and, consistent with the results of Krause (1992) and Krause and Dawis (1992), psychological factors are important in the understanding of short- and long-term adjustment.

While individuals' background, experiences, beliefs, and personality play key roles in their *disabled experience*, another influence is the type of motivation used by the person's family and rehabilitation team. Ken used the example of the individuals portrayed in the book, *Options*, as being a particular type of motivator. He further said,

> It's one thing to give a ray of hope, everybody needs that; but it's quite another to indicate they can get up and walk again someday. They should build confidence without building hopes so high that people expect they can be completely normal. Assistive devices can help you,

but they're not going to enable you to walk or to get back the use of your hands. . . A lot of it is just time.

It is also the importance of looking beyond the physical aspects of rehabilitation to the psychosocial needs of the person.

There is perhaps no better example of the healing value of time and the importance of psychosocial readiness than Butch's experience.

Butch, 1991

Approaching Butch's house once again, I no longer had any feelings of apprehension or anxiety. Everything looked about the same; but this time I noticed food scattered in one area of the driveway for the squirrels and birds and the van sitting in a different part of the driveway than usual. As I was getting out of the car, a door opened and Butch's mother gestured for me to come in. Her now familiar warm greeting was followed by a few minutes of friendly conversation. Then I got on the elevator to take myself up to Butch's annex.

Once at the door, Butch responded to my knock with his booming but cheerful, 'C'mon in.' Upon entering, I was shocked to come face-to-face with the biggest stuffed buffalo head I had ever seen. Butch, eclipsed by the thing and chuckling, peered out from around it and proceeded to tell me just how he had come to own this furry masterpiece. Then he pointed out his other recent acquisitions: a bear skin rug, a ram's head, and a five foot carved wooden bear. These were nothing, however, compared to the 10 x 6 1/2 foot latch hooked rug on the wall over the sofa. It portrayed The Last Supper and Butch had created it in just 57 days as a Christmas present for his mother.

Butch's life is now a busy one. He is nearing the end of the process of making a new power wheelchair. 'I got together all the parts, welded them, and am doing the whole thing myself.'

He goes out quite frequently. 'There isn't a mall in the area I don't have memorized.' He travels around primarily with family, but has a friend with whom he double-dated with this past summer to go to a rock concert — his first ever. He does not yet dine out, however, as 'I go into terrible spasms after I eat and who wants to see that?'

Overall, Butch says that 'I enjoy myself more now. You know, it's been 3,328 days since my injury and it just got boring sitting here doing nothin.'

3,328 days — and counting.

Coping and Non-coping

In Beatrice Wright's classic text, *Physical disability: A Psychological Approach* (1960), considerable attention is devoted to coping and non-coping which are defined as follows:

> Coping - [Seeing] the difficulties associated with a disability as something that [can] be faced in some way or overcome...[focusing] on the adjustable aspects... coping with the difficulties rather than managing because of blissful ignorance or pretense (p.59).

> Succumbing (non-coping) - [Seeing] difficulties as a quagmire through which there [is] no path. Perhaps one doesn't even seek a path, for one is so consumed with the suffering of the disabled state that one is dragged down by despair (p.59).

People who **cope** emphasize what they can do and seek to satisfy achievement and affiliation needs; persons who **succumb** focus on what they cannot do. People who **cope** pursue opportunities; people who **succumb** are more passive, downplay their competence, and distrust the opportunities presented to them; **coping behaviors** are employed to overcome limitations — through further education, the development of new skills, and the use of assistive technologies; **succumbing** is characterized by a resignation to and a concentration on limitations.

Cycles of Hope and Despair

Coping involves achieving or maintaining control. When a person experiences a severe trauma such as a spinal cord injury, a major disequilibrium occurs. This occurs on a group level, as for a family, and for the individual with the new disability. Some individuals with recently acquired disabilities, who experience a major change in lifestyle, may not have had earlier experiences and exposures essential to the development of decision-making, responsibility, and self-control. Individuals born with cerebral palsy were rarely given such opportunities. Therefore, a new or additional disability, deteriorating health, a change in one's famlily or financial situation, can overtax a person's psychological resources. While crises are difficult for everyone to handle, they can be especially so for persons with disabilities who have not had a range of opportunities for managing a variety of situations.

Coping can vary between the extremes of "phenomenal success" to marginal coping. *Non-coping*, too, varies between complete withdrawal, helplessness, and hopelessness to maintaining marginal functioning that develops over time to coping and adjustment. As we develop and mature, we formulate new strategies for goal achievement. When they work and we are successful, it appears we are coping. Should our strategies fail us for a time, we may exhibit non-coping behaviors. Coping and non-coping people display significant differences that vary according to the setting in which they find themselves and the kind and amount of personal, professional, social and financial resources available to them.

As we saw in Jim's case, one may experience "phenomenal success" at one point in time and marginal coping, or even succumbing, at another. And examples abound of *succumbing* persons who later become *copers*.

In 1986, Butch appeared to be *non-coping* to his OVR counselor, Chris. Yet, anyone familiar with persons with disabilities knows that a random sample will reflect as wide a range of diversity as is found in the population as a whole. There will be pessimists and optimists, religious and non-religious individuals,Type A personalities and passive persons, angry people and easygoing persons, people with a good social support network and people in social conflict, people who are denying the facts of their disability, people who have actively sought out all the information they can about their disability, and so on. To look at the personality of each of these individuals and accurately predict who will be a future "rehabilitation success" and who will not is impossible. To think there is conclusive evidence for predictable emotional and mental patterns in coping and adjustment is to do a tremendous disservice to all persons who have a disability.

This was precisely one of Susan Sontag's points in her classic essay, *Illness as Metaphor* (1978) and in her later work, *AIDS and its Metaphors* (1989). Sontag argues that as soon as one assigns control to the individual for his or her disease, then the ill person becomes responsible both for falling ill *and* for the failure to get well again.

Still, succumbing to a lifestyle of dependence is certainly a different statement from a spirited determination and drive to overcome obstacles to achievement and independence. To help a person move from withdrawal and hopelessness to adjustment and coping requires attention to physical, social, developmental, and psychological/personal factors, but in a studied and cautious manner. To omit the effects of time and everyone's attempts to think about and understand their disability ignores the positive growth principle implied in Maslow's hierarchy which was presented as the context for the discussion in this chapter.

Summary

Figure 6-1 shows how assistive technology use both influences and is influenced by a person's view of *quality of life, rehabilitation success* and the *disabled experience*. These in turn affect and are affected by physiological, psychological and psychosocial "determiners of disability." Achieving the best possible match of person and technology is now a key element of individual need satisfaction and, therefore, it has become a crucial component of the rehabilitation process.

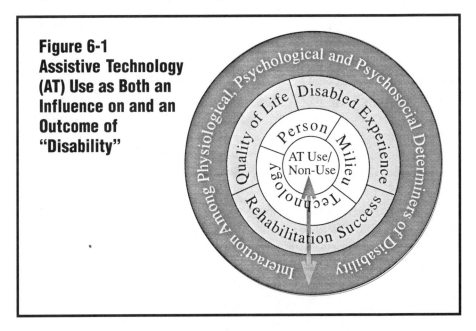

Figure 6-1 Assistive Technology (AT) Use as Both an Influence on and an Outcome of "Disability"

REFERENCE NOTES

[1]   This formulation of Maslow's hierarchy was modified by Root (1970) and is used in the text by Gage & Berliner (1992).

[2]   Recent news accounts have reported that "exotic dancing" has had a resurgence in popularity, which is attributed to fear of AIDS and a desire for experiences which make a person feel attractive.

CHAPTER SEVEN

Dilemmas, Challenges and Opportunities

> Why, then the world's mine oyster,
> Which I with sword will open.
> Shakespeare

Carolyn Vash (1983) believes the pivotal issue determining whether or not an assistive technology is used is "the degree to which a device promotes accomplishment of life tasks which the consumer sees as important." Before assistive device use can enhance a person's quality of life, there must be a social climate which values enhanced capability and a "psychological readiness" for technology use on the part of the individual with a disability.

In the past couple of decades, there has been an explosion in the number and types of medical, assistive, and learning technologies designed to help persons survive and overcome severe limitations in functioning from physical illness and disability. Accompanying the increasing availability of these technologies has been a steadily growing concern over their appropriate prescription, selection and use.

THE NEED FOR A MODEL WHEN MATCHING A PERSON AND A TECHNOLOGY (MPT)

Ultimately, the goal of rehabilitation professionals is to match an individual with an assistive device that will enhance the person's capabilities and quality of life. Regardless of the type of device under consideration, an individual will be either a user or non-user. But people can vary within the categories of use or non-use: Non-use can be due to device abandoment or the avoidance of a device altogether — e.g. a person will not show up for an evaluation/fitting or will not purchase it. Use can be full-time and done willingly, or partial and done reluctantly. Partial use most frequently occurs with persons whose device use is not optional or where a person will use a device in one environment but not another.

Need determines use

We know that the highest rate of assistive technology use occurs a) the more limited an individual's functioning and b) when viable alternatives to use do not exist or are not available. For example, everyone mentioned in this book uses a wheelchair; the only alternative for them would be a lack of mobility. A person with CP who has little or no intelligible speech will be a more frequent user of a computerized communication system than someone who has difficulty with only certain words. Thus, the degree to which an assistive device is essential for functioning determines its use. As a former founding director of a rehabilitation unit said to me,

> It seems the more the device is needed for self-care and independence both in and outside of the home, the more it is used. A classic example involves almost 100% prosthetic arm use by someone without any arms, but if one arm is normal, use falls drastically.

And, according to Kate,

> [Non-use of communication devices] is due in part to the fact that communication is a very fast process and no current device provides the same speed — although some are getting close. It depends on the person and what that person wants to say and how adept she or he is at saying it. I know if I had to spell out every word I wanted to say, especially after having a normal rate of speech, I'm not going to say very much and I'm not going to use very long sentences. With a device, communication comes across as terse and all sorts of subtleties are lost.

As the examples of Chuck and Brian showed in Chapter One, not only do more severely disabled individuals require more equipment, but more expensive equipment.

The myriad influences on the use or non-use of more optional assistive technologies can be organized into a model, the MPT model, as follows:

1. The characteristics of the **M**ilieu (environment and psychosocial setting) in which the assistive technology is used,

2. Pertinent features of the individual's **P**ersonality and temperament, and

3. The salient characteristics of the assistive **T**echnology itself.

Figure 7-1 graphically displays this "Matching Person and Technology (MPT)" model and shows how positive and negative influences within each of the areas will result in situations varying between device use or non-use. Figure 7-2 then organizes the characteristics of persons who

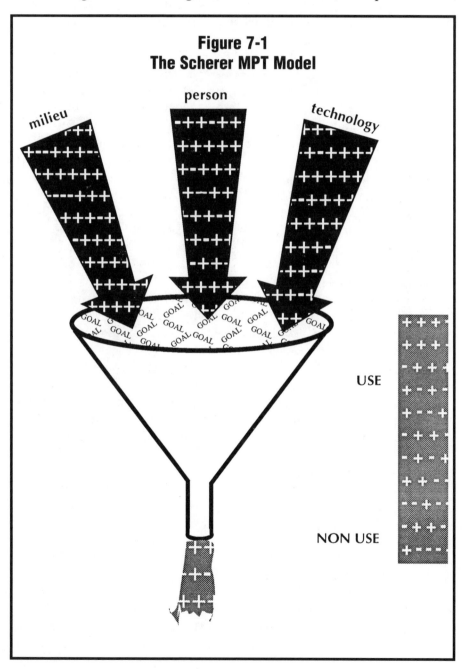

Figure 7-1
The Scherer MPT Model

Figure 7.2
Assistive Technology Influences

	Milieu	Personality	Technology
U S E Optimal	Support from family/peers/ employer Realistic expectations of family/ employer Setting/environment fully supports and rewards use	Proud to use device Motivated Cooperative Optimistic Good coping skills Patient Self-disciplined Generally positive life experiences Has the skills to use the device Perceives discrepancy between desired and current situation	Goal achieved with no pain, fatigue or stress Compatible with/enhances the use of other technologies Is safe, reliable, easy to use and maintain Has the desired transportability No better options currently available
Partial/ Reluctant	Pressure for use from either family/peers/employer Assistance often not available Setting/environment discourages use or makes use awkward	Embarrassed to use device Unmotivated Impatient/impulsive Unrealistic expectations Low self-esteem Somewhat intimidated by technology Technology partially or occasionally fits with lifestyle Deficits in skills needed for use	Goal not fully achieved or with discomfort/strain Requires a lot of set-up Interferes somewhat with the use of other technologies Device is inefficient Other options to device use exist

Figure 7.2 (cont.)
Assistive Technology Influences

N **O** **N** **U** **S** **E**	**Avoidance**	Lack of support from either family/peers/employer Unrealistic expectations of others Assistance not available Setting/environment disallows or prevents use	Person doesn't want it Embarrassed to use device Depressed Unmotivated Uncooperative Withdrawn Intimidated by technology Many changes required in lifestyle Does not have skills for use	*Perceived* lack of goal achievement or too much strain/discomfort in use Requires a lot of set-up Perceived or determined to be incompatible with the use of other technologies Too expensive Long delay for delivery Other options to device use exist
	Abandonment	Lack of support from either family/peers/employer Setting/environment discourages or makes use awkward Requires assistance that is not available	Embarrassed to use device Depressed Low self-esteem Hostile/angry Withdrawn Resistant Poor socialization and coping skills Many changes in lifestyle with device use Lacks skills to use device and training is not available	Goal not achieved and/or discomfort/strain in use Is incompatible with the use of other technologies Has been outgrown Is difficult to use Device is inefficient Repairs/service not timely or affordable Other options to use became available

optimally use devices or who use them partially or reluctantly as compared to those who abandon the use of them or who avoid their use altogether.

The use of the MPT model can provide both a broad and in-depth profile of where persons may be at a particular point in time with their devices. For example, a person may look like a partial or reluctant device user as far as the **Milieu**, but appear to be an optimal user according to the characteristics listed for **Personality** and **Technology**. Thus, the **Milieu** of use may need some intervention or modification for the person to gain maximum satisfaction and functional gain from the device.

Assistive device use is interactive: an alteration in one set of factors will have an effect on the others. For example, optimal use of one assistive device may likely lead to enthusiasm for trying another device, improved self-confidence, and a wider social milieu. It is also the case that a person can be in one category with one device at a particular point in time and be in another with a second device at the same point in time. Sometimes, the introduction of a new device can make the use of an existing one more complicated or cumbersome. It is likely that as time goes on, device compatibility or incompatibility will be a growing area of concern. We've become aware that a "fatal threshold" can be reached when a system composed of one or more devices has an additive effect, resulting in frustration and overload for a person and even such difficulties as *repetitive motion injuries*.

Characteristics of the Milieu

Consumers of assistive technology services include persons with disabilities (primary consumers) and their family members and caretakers (secondary consumers). It is important to involve at the outset all who will be affected by the assistive technology, keeping in mind the function to which the technology will be put and the environment in which it will operate and be used. According to one rehabilitation engineer,

> The crucial step is to have the individual try it, to go through the routine of actually using the equipment or mimicking the use of that equipment. Usually with a device comes a need for extra room. If the individual is not able to use it, you can look for other alternatives, see if there's need for further modification, etc. Sometimes you may have to start all over again. It's a man-machine interface where you're trying to get that

individual with that particular disability able to operate a device in one or more environments. Many times I feel more like a social worker. You become an investigator, a detective. You find out what the different alternatives are within the constraints.

> The value of offering trial periods before finalizing a technology selection is very important. The consumer must try the device in the actual situation of use (home, work, school).

One of the most common reasons for the non-use or reluctant use of an assistive technology is that it was forced upon the person by family members or therapists. This is very common with children. Just as some families will resist the use of technological assistance, many will purchase anything they believe will help their child only to discover that the child either does not want to use it or cannot use it. A children's hospital did a six-month follow-up study and discovered that 75% of the devices prescribed were not being used.

> Primary and secondary consumers need to have information about the advantages of a technology and know why, when and under what circumstances it will be most useful.

Milieu Factors Influencing Device Use

Exposure and opportunity. Factors such as environmental accommodations, available resources (e.g. private insurance for specialized treatment, availability of personal assistance) and special opportunities (e.g. placement in a rehabilitation center with the newest equipment) are also important **Milieu** characteristics. Often, rehabilitation can seem like a "one-shot chance," as expressed by Chuck:

> I wish it was set up so that you could go home for a year and then come back. Just so you could get more work done in some areas and strengthen points you want to work on and where you'd have a therapist who would give you ideas on how to make things better at home. I mean,

don't go just cold turkey. Usually once you're done with rehab, that's it, you're done with rehab. . . . But it would be great to have that individual help after a year or so.

> Follow-up or repeat visits help consumers further refine/integrate the use of a device.

Socialization, particularly for those with congenital disabilities, plays an important role, as Kate describes:

> Many of our people with cerebral palsy always had someone to take care of them. They never had to cope with things and they haven't developed those skills, they never learned them. Also, they tend to have low opinions of their abilities — 'I can't feed myself,' 'I can't do the simplest things other people take for granted.' To be a successful user of a device requires patience and perseverance. Suffocating families and institutions sap individuals of that, of enthusiasm, the hope that something new and exciting can still happen. When you see an assistive device as an opportunity to better your life and situation, then you're willing to pay the price of a long, tiring, frustrating trial-and-error period of learning. If the desire and perseverance aren't there, the frustration is too great and after a short trial the device is shoved in the closet because it was too much of a hassle or it was just too overwhelming.

Some of the most frequent problems encountered in the use of communication systems, in fact, include the individual's lack of such fundamental communication skills as topic initiation and conversational turn-taking (Creech, 1990; Bjorck-Akesson, 1990; Musselwhite, 1990).

> A peer user of the same or similar device can be of tremendous support and assistance during the trial period of device use.

Expectations. The attitudes of others and their expectations of the client, as expressed through intimate interactions or through exposure to the values of society as a whole, can have a profound influence on persons and their expectations of themselves. What may seem to be a vital task to one person may be of small value to another. The self concept, motivation and personal aspirations of an individual are shaped by social interactions and support that serve to control positive personal regard, resources and opportunities. Other influences on a person's achievement of rehabilitation goals are the characteristics of the goal itself (explicit, close to where the person's performance currently is so as to maximize the chance it will be achieved, and not too difficult) and whether the experience of success or failure accompanied the process of goal achievement.

> For new users especially, it is helpful to take things one step at a time, rewarding each accomplishment.

Social support. It is important to distinguish persons who report being *lonely* from those who are *isolated*. *Loneliness* is a subjective sense of being alone, even when surrounded by significant others; *isolation*, on the other hand, implies a dearth of social contacts. *Loneliness* requires a more psychological intervention whereas *isolation* suggests a need for increased social opportunities which may be greatly facilitated by assistive technology use.

An acquired disability often places sudden strains on family relationships and social resources. When the support network is altered, the person may experience both psychological and physical distress, which can lead to a further disorganization, deterioration, and disintegration of the social support system.

Not all positive social ties are supportive of assistive technology use. When effective support is given, it is important to know under what conditions the aid was actually given — i.e., what was said or done to attract that positive aid.

Assistive device users tend to have more social support than non-users. For example, their families built ramps and modified the family home, or their employer held a job for them. Family reluctance to have the person return home unaided, stable family relations, and being the person responsible for family maintenance, were all positively associated with assistive technology use.

The individual's cultural identity and the values and norms of that culture should be considered. For example, persons who wear hearing aids are viewed as rejecting Deaf Culture. There may also be cultural (and/or age) barriers to help-seeking in general.

In addition to the need to keep all of the above factors in mind when matching a person with an assistive technology, Thomason (1990) points out the need to consider the physical environments of use. When planning to equip rural Native Americans with assistive devices, he advises the consideration of terrain, the availability of electricity, etc.

> Asking the individual about his or her social and material support, including cultural preferences, is an important part of the assessment process for Milieu influences on use/non-use.

Characteristics of the Person

Brooks and Redden (1986) surveyed the membership of the Resource Group of Scientists and Engineers with Disabilities (a sub-group of the American Association for the Advancement of Science). Their findings highlight the complex interrelationships that exist among disability-related characteristics, the particular social settings in which the person is involved, an individual's anticipated public response to the device, the person's attitudes toward the device and view of a particular device as being helpful or restricting.

Technical comfort. The assumption that all people with disabilities have the desire to effectively utilize a computer-operated device is not an accurate one. Women in our society have traditionally received little exposure to technical perspectives and tend to be uninformed about computers and disinterested in the complex and sophisticated products of rehabilitation engineering efforts (Littrell, 1991; Scherer, 1991b). Non-technically oriented males, on the other hand, can feel even more threatened by technological devices since they may feel an additional assault to their egos because they lack skills that are traditionally male objects of interest.

Persons without the education, socialization or exposure to the use of a computer can exhibit anxiety when faced with one. Being anxious makes it more difficult for them to learn the skills to operate it. In addition to feeling anxious around technological devices, people often have a distrust of them, which is frequently borne out (as Ann and Linda showed in Chapter Six) by such things as a stalled power wheelchair.

Enders (1984) notes that among the general population of persons with disabilities there are individuals who are intimidated by high-tech assistive devices (technophobes) and, alternately, there are those who want only the high-tech ones (technophiles). If devices are pushed onto the technophobic person, the devices often end up being unused or abandoned. But, according to Enders, an equally nonproductive situation results if the technophile is given everything he or she requests — then the glitzy and innovative aspects may take precedence over the functional ones and a device will only be used until the next new innovation comes along.

Individuals who appear to be technophobic are persons who typically have not been exposed to technologies. For them, the potential of achieving limited gains through the use of an assistive device is not worth the anxiety or discomfort involved in its use. Kate notes in the following statement that this situation will no doubt change as people become increasingly exposed to technologies at very young ages.

> Maybe if there were some dramatic technical changes that made a quantum leap in convenience or appropriateness... Either the device is unsophisticated enough to really make a difference or it's so sophisticated that people can't or don't want to deal with the complexity of it. I think you can argue the case that if it truly makes a difference for an individual, then the person will use it.
>
> I think younger people coming along are going to do much better. Most children with disabilities today are exposed to computers at a fairly young age. So a computer to them is not like a strange box that they don't know how to operate. It's no more strange than their wheelchair or eyeglasses. For the people who are seeing their first computer at the age of fifty, and who managed for fifty years without it, the device doesn't make a significant enough difference to warrant all that effort to learn to use it. This is a transition time. In thirty years it will all be commonplace and everyone will have equipment.

When feeling anxious or technophobic about the use of a technology in public, interactions with others can become more strained, especially since assistive devices serve as signs of disability and set a person apart as being different. As Chuck mentioned in Chapter One, they can both physically and socially separate persons with disabilities from those without disabilities. Since a person's self-esteem and self-image are built up over time through interactions with other persons, the presence of assistive devices can define those interactions and ultimately the elements of a person's self-image.

> To build the user's self-confidence and confidence with the device, ensure each training session ends as a successful experience with user mastery and control of the device. Never let a session end in failure or on a frustrating note.

Cognitive abilities and aptitude. People differ in their aptitudes to effectively use assistive devices. The more sophisticated any device is, the more complicated the training may be in how to use that device. If an individual cannot read or spell, then a computerized device that relies on reading/spelling as input would probably be inappropriate for that person without a good deal of remedial work or other training; nonverbal, pictorial devices may be preferable. If a device requires more than a two-step command, a person who does not understand or manage sequence well, who is highly distractable, or who has a very short memory span will be handicapped by that device. So will the person who has been given a device that requires the development of unusual or new skills or that requires a large amount of conscious effort to control it. As explained by one rehabilitation professional,

> It is not helpful to ask more of a person than he or she can realistically be expected to deliver. For example, a high school graduate with fourth grade reading and math skills will not become a capable clerical person until he or she shows at least a seventh grade ability. So I don't buy this person a word processor prematurely.

Unlike Maggie, many persons her age born with cerebral palsy lack the basic educational background to take advantage of the opportunities afforded them by technological advances, particularly computerized devices. The emphasis technology places on cognitive and perceptual capabilities, as opposed to motor and physical skills, has opened many opportunities for persons with physical disabilities but has created some barriers for persons with cognitive or perceptual disabilities. For individuals with cognitive, perceptual, and learning disabilities, a multi-sensory approach to teaching and providing feedback works best as computer use involves the person's auditory, visual and tactile senses. For mild deficits, it is also helpful to supply the user with memory aids such as cards listing the sequence of steps to follow in commonly used procedures.

> A multi-sensory approach to teaching and providing feedback works best for everyone. Involve the auditory, visual and tactile senses as much as possible. Consider using memory aids such as cards listing the sequence of steps in commonly used procedures.

Personality traits. Many spinal cord injured persons find it difficult to adapt to a computer's discipline, especially those, as Chris put it, who had been "more at home with their bodies than with their minds." On the other hand, many people with cerebral palsy characterized as quiet and passive often adapt to the computer's structure easily and willingly.

Device use is more acceptable when options are available and the person can exercise choice. While a wheelchair is not usually an optional piece of equipment for a person, the type and number of wheelchairs a person has *is* under more individual control. Chuck has two wheelchairs, one for traveling outdoors and one he uses only for inside the house. When Chris was working, she had a wheelchair at home and both a wheelchair and a scooter at work. But for many persons, multiple wheelchairs remain only a hope, as noted by one woman with CP:

> It would be nice if the [electric wheelchair] could be folded-up and put in the trunk of a car. More streamlined, smaller, not as heavy. I'd rather be able to use a manual chair. Vehicles are not adapted for electric chairs. Because I can't ride in many vehicles and need to be bodily carried in and out of cars, I get left out of a lot of things I'd like to do, things I'd like to do with my husband. I can't go to all the places he can [her husband uses a manual wheelchair].

Judgment and preference. Many persons prefer to use an attendant or what they themselves have, however limited, as opposed to a mechanical replacement for their limited functions. Too, consumers can differ in their judgments of the potential functional gains assistive devices offer them, as the following quote from Kate indicates.

> One person with cerebral palsy, for example, may determine that a device will not improve her speech intelligibility enough to warrant its use, while another equally affected individual may see a device as not only desirable, but indispensable. I am working with a person now who found her own balance. She has made very effective use of a small, portable, communication device by using it to augment a word here and there.

Assistive technologies are used when consumers have goals and see the device as valuable to goal achievement. Device selection that is user driven will ego-invest the person in using that device.

Adjustment and Outlook. Different physical disabilities are associated with different complications, courses of treatment and rehabilitation. For example, an individual born with a disability has likely incorporated the disability into the self-image and has accepted the disability and lifestyle modifications it may require. Individuals with cerebral palsy tend to see assistive technologies as opening up entire new vistas and making available new experiences and opportunities.

For persons experiencing a spinal cord injury in early adulthood or a stroke in middle-age, assistive technologies may be viewed as reminders of the independent functioning they have lost. Their disabilities can represent a major life change requiring modification in the person's basic identity and established ways of doing things. This can be met with resentment, as Chuck indicated in Chapter One:

> Your basic style doesn't change just because you're in a wheelchair and the only things you can move are from the neck up.

Research by Rohe and Krause (1992) has shown that the occupational and avocational interest of 79 men with spinal cord injuries remained stable in spite of their injury. There was no decrease of interest in physically demanding and adventuresome activities.

People who do have the same or similar disabilities attach different meanings to what has happened to them and what their future is likely to be like. Pre-existing temperament and ways of coping are just two factors that can influence the length and quality of the recovery and rehabilitation process and adjustment.

As Ken said in Chapter Six, the process of adjustment to a spinal cord injury may include periods of depression and pessimism during which time a person may have a negative outlook about his or her future. It frequently takes persons with spinal cord injuries seven or more years to come to terms with their disabilities. Many refer to the drastic adjustments they must make by talking, as Brian does, in terms of their "two lives." Often the "second life" means one has adopted a different lifestyle and outlook.

Individuals who use assistive devices say they have goals they want to pursue, believe obstacles to their independence can be overcome, tend to focus on expanding their capabilities, see opportunities rather than limitations and believe they control their quality of life. Device users are not easily discouraged; in fact, they enjoy challenge. As noted by a former director of a rehabilitation unit who is now the director of a medical division for a large corporation:

> It appears that assistive device use depends on the person's decision that 1) he or she was going to perform a given task and 2) that it could not be done without a device. Often, time, learning, doing, and yearning is necessary before that decision is made. Systems (and people) which force the decision on the person prematurely are flawed.

Attending to and monitoring the self-esteem of the client is important in the timing of assistive technology recommendations. Assistive technology use requires an admission to the self that one cannot, and possibly never will, do a functional task on one's own. It requires admitting a loss, weakness, or deficit and this can be distressing. A push for pre-mature device use can be a mistake for those individuals who, as Butch said, "first need time to get used to just the thought of it." Both Butch and Ken eventually "got fed up with doing nothing;" for them, boredom was a motivator out of the state of stuck. Later, a desire for regained control and independence led them to enhanced assistive technology use.

Many individuals with disabilities harbor hopes for a cure for their disability or say they are waiting for the mass availability of prematurely-touted experimental devices that they see as superior to those currently available. Such hopes often serve to hinder their rehabilitation.

Counseling may be indicated for those persons who are angry and depressed and who didn't learn how to make choices ("learned helplessness"). Users can be given control by providing them with information that enables them to predict occurrences in advance so they can prepare for them.

Characteristics of the Assistive Technology

Batavia, Dillard and Phillips (1990), at the National Rehabilitation Hospital Rehabilitation Engineering Center in Washington, DC, are investigating the abandonment of assistive technologies through telephone surveys with persons with disabilities. Their preliminary findings indicate that the reasons people abandoned their devices can be grouped into three main categories:

1. It did not improve independent functioning.
2. Servicing and repair were difficult to obtain and/or were very expensive.
3. The device was too difficult to use, performed unreliably or required too much assistance from another person.

When the use of a device interferes with other activities or need satisfaction, it may be viewed as ineffective and then becomes abandoned. When the device itself was satisfactory, survey respondents often reported changed priorities or needs that led to the abandonment or replacement of a device.

The results of a follow-up study of the use of mobility devices by 196 patients of the Children's Hospital at Stanford (conducted from 1975-1978) show that several trade-offs need to be kept in mind: for example, between the unattractiveness of a device and certain functional gains, and that an individual's long term gains sometimes require short-term stress, e.g. the family initially will have to build a ramp and (re)arrange transportation.

Design factors. Bowe notes that assistive technologies have a high rate of use when they are lightweight and portable, easy to use and set up, are cost effective to obtain and maintain, and are the same as or similar to devices used by the non-disabled population. Disincentives to device use include the lack of the above as well as user frustration with their speed, size or complexity (Bowe, 1984; 1988).

The flexibility of devices and the degree to which they can accommodate the addition of other devices are also important. The increased practice of integrating multiple devices so they can be controlled by a single input device often results in a more streamlined appearance, but just as often has resulted in situations of "cognitive overload."

Devices are unlikely to be used if they "never seem to be there when needed," are seen as "not worth all the effort," do not have enough practical applications, and create discomfort or inconvenience. When caretakers view devices as requiring too much work and effort, they will not use them. Kate provides an example:

> Another point parents make is that the machine is always in the wrong room. They move the child or the child moves around and they go for the device and it's not there. 'Oh well, forget it then.'

When asked his opinion of the factors that should be considered in the design of assistive technologies in the future, a rehabilitation engineer responded as follows:

> Encourage the development of smaller, and not so cumbersome models of the equipment. The portability and packaging, outer looks, of the device should be as aesthetically pleasing as possible. Devices should be non-visible. We should maximize the use of current components used in industry in order for non-disabled people to be able to identify with device users more. I also want to highlight the need for streamlining designs to try to make them 'acceptable' or even 'attractive' to persons who do not have a disability.

The following are some principles of "unusual product design":
1. Provide multi-sensory cues and messages;
2. Try to have as many controls as possible operate through gross movements;
3. Reduce device complexity;
4. Provide adjustable interfaces;
5. Prevent accidental activation of key controls.

Maggie's speech therapist, in discussing the design of communication devices, offers an example of the social aspects of device inconvenience:

> Socially and interpersonally, there can be difficulties. No piece of equipment on its own can bring social acceptance of the person. In fact, equipment can present its own social problems. For example, when a person uses a certain kind of typing device, the listener has to wait there for a very long time. Sometimes when they see the user approaching them, there's almost an avoidance reaction, 'Oh, I don't want to get caught.'

A person with one or two hearing aids, or with a communication system, becomes personally involved to a greater extent than a person with an impersonal environmental control system. Levels of comfort with use, even around family members, vary widely. Feelings of being conspicuous are compounded when assistive technologies are designed to look functional and utilitarian for funding sources and, as a result, leave many users feeling deviant and stigmatized. Even rehabilitation engineers acknowledge the potential stigmatizing effect of current devices. For example:

> In some cases I've seen very good ideas developed, but they're so large and cumbersome that it takes hours for a person to set it up. Too, aesthetically [size and shape, etc.] they may be so unusual that the person doesn't feel comfortable using it. People usually opt for the easy way out. If something has to be set up in a special way, if it's somewhat complex and it takes some time to do it, those are deterrents to use for all but the super-motivated. How would we like to be able to speak only after our device was set up? And we wouldn't want to have to wait to talk until our device was repaired.

A device that looks unusual and does not meet the user's real needs and desires is one that will end up stored in the closet.

While the individual's milieu needs to be adjusted to the person's functional capabilities, the person's capabilities also have to be enhanced in order to ensure successful integration. We need to take advantage of device flexibility and available training options to accommodate differences among users.

Service delivery. Assistive technologies are not used if other support services are not there. For example, a specially-equipped van is less useful when there are no handicapped parking spaces. Homebound persons and those in remote and rural areas may be unfamiliar with many devices because they haven't been exposed to them and may not have access to peers or trained professionals to help them learn to use them properly.

It is not uncommon for persons with new hearing aids to abandon their use when they discover that "perfect hearing" is not restored and they have not received training in the limitations of hearing aids nor in communication management. Yet, the technical aspects of rehabilitation have become so complex that specialists have had to de-emphasize many of the related psychosocial aspects. The curriculum for technologists leaves precious little room for courses in psychology, other social sciences and the huamnities.

While technical specialists may lack skills in human service delivery, rehabilitation professionals who do not perceive themselves as technically skilled may avoid learning about new technologies, may downplay the usefulness of the devices, and not present them as viable options. If professionals have had unpleasant experiences matching consumers with technologies, or participated in too many overly technical workshops, they may have become soured on continuing education programs designed to increase, update or broaden their own technical skills.

Consumers themselves may be unwilling to request training or other assistance. While many remain uninformed about the options available to them, others are not accustomed to being assertive and may hesitate to ask for the assistance to which they are entitled.

Training in device use is very important, as Kate notes, for both users — and their family members and caretakers:

> The technology itself requires *a lot* of training. To train not only the user but the caregivers because the caregivers have to learn how to problem solve if there's a sudden malfunction of the equipment. We also need to start training those informal technicians, such as the neighborhood electrician, who are called upon to fabricate and trouble shoot devices.

As important, Kate said, is the availability of a back-up system:

> Technology brings more breakdowns and frustration as a result of that. Sometimes the down time for repairs can be very long so a person needs access to a back-up system of some sort.

Donna, Maggie's speech therapist, made a similar point:

> Assistive device use should only be encouraged and recommended
> when the potential user can tolerate technology breakdown or down-
> time and utilize other compensatory skills and techniques. It also
> frequently occurs that a school will supply a communication system of
> some type for a student's use that has to be left there at the end of the day.
> Then the student has to go home and use a different means of commu-
> nicating.

In addition, people develop and change. Unless they have on-going
access to rehabilitation professionals, they may stop using a device when
all it may require to become useful again is some small adjustment or
modification. Children, in particular, outgrow devices (either physically
or developmentally) and need to be able to go to rehabilitation centers for
upgrades or more developmentally appropriate devices. Even in rehabilitation centers, however, it can occur that therapists with close ties to
certain vendors, or who have had success with a particular device with
one or two clients, will prescribe that device too frequently, believing it
to have wider application than it in fact has.

Funding for Devices. Another difficulty with assistive devices is the
current bureaucratic procedures that must be followed to obtain funding
for equipment. A lengthy wait can sometimes make a device become
inappropriate from the time it was recommended to the time it is
received. Kate provides an example:

> Any negative is vastly overridden by the positives, but technology is
> expensive and outside funding takes time — six to eight months. This
> can be very frustrating, particularly if the gap is large between the time
> the person is exposed to a piece of technology, tries it out, and is able to
> have it. I personally have mixed feelings because I think the Government
> should look carefully at these expenditures, yet, a lot can happen in six
> to eight months. The person can change physically and functionally,
> developmentally, a lot can happen.

Vince, a rehabilitation engineer, highlighted the importance of appealing
to funding sources when he said:

> A lot of devices are turned down for funding because they're not
> considered a necessity. A lot of that is because the funding agency

doesn't look at the complete situation. An environmental control unit in a person's house can pay for itself very quickly when it gives access to a telephone. Help can be called when needed, and it reduces the number of hours an attendant has to be there. And I don't know if that's looked at all the time. Many times requests for powered wheelchairs get turned down, but mobility is something that can open up a lot of options for a person: maybe they can get back to work, produce their own income.

There appears to be a growing "prosperity gap" between those who can and those who cannot obtain certain kinds of assistive devices. Butch gives an example:

> This one guy I know is so limited he can't even answer the telephone. He could use an environmental control system but he can't afford one and no one will give him one. For him to have to sit there and know one guy's getting it and he isn't — it really aggravates him. He's lower functioning because of his financial situation and the gap between him and this other guy with an environmental system has widened as a result. Devices are great when they're equally available to everyone, but when they're not they sure do tip the scales. So now he stays stoned all the time. What kind of life is that?

Funding for assistive technologies is problematic. Not only are limited funds available, but agency policies often work at cross purposes so that many persons "fall between the cracks." If a person is unemployed, does not qualify for vocational or educational assistance, cannot obtain private health insurance and is not medically eligible for Medicaid or Medicare, there are few remaining options other than university based programs with research funding, and private philanthropy.

According to a rehabilitation engineer, high functioning individuals can be served at less expense than those with more severe disabilities who are low functioning. Since funding, trained personnel, and equipment are limited, the general practice is to utilize the available pool of resources to help as many high functioning persons as possible maintain or enhance their functioning rather than exhaust already limited resources on relatively few low functioning individuals. This presents yet another dilemma: Persons not in the labor force may be unable to get the equipment they need in order to be employable, yet an overemphasis on assistive technologies in the workplace sends a signal to persons with disabilities that they cannot expect to be employed unless they can do everything a non-disabled employee can do (Perlman & Hansen, 1989).

It reinforces the attitude on the part of employers and fellow workers that people with disabilities present difficult problems requiring high-tech solutions. As noted in an issue of *Newsletter for Industry* (published by the President's Committee on the Employment of People with Disabilities), the strips of wire under the carpeting in airports which give audio guidance signals to blind travelers equipped with a special receiver lead people to believe that blind people can't adapt to the world around them without such accommodations. On the other hand, an airport guidance system, for an employer who believes mobility is a central problem for blind employees, may serve to show that blind persons can be in jobs which require travel.

Cost Effectiveness. The cost effectiveness of assistive technologies is a primary concern as we move into the 21st century. If a low cost device has only limited uses or requires the same number of man hours to use as the next cheapest alternative, or if it provides no gain in independence, then it's not cost effective. But a very expensive device, such as a Kurzweil reading machine for persons who are blind, may pay for itself in 2 to 5 years just in the amount of money saved in readers' fees. Beyond this, the Kurzweil machine allows for greater independence and flexibility than a reader and its varied applications and capabilities make it a quite reasonable — even bargain — investment.

Another example of the kinds of trade-offs that figure into the calculations of cost-efficient and cost-effective approaches to rehabilitation is provided by Dudek (1985). For $500 a 30 year old male who is a dual leg amputee can have a manual wheelchair which may result in a gain of 15% of the lower limit of "normal mobility." His personal care and transportation needs over a thirty year lifespan yield a total cost of about $420,500. A power wheelchair with a cost of $15,000 could give him 30% of the lower limit of normal mobility and he may then only need a part-time attendant which would drop the 30-year lifespan costs to $375,000. If this individual is provided with artificial limbs and therapy he may regain 75% of the lower limit of "normal mobility" at a cost of $45,000. He will have considerable autonomy, and would require limited personal care and could drive an adapted automobile at a total cost over thirty years of $90,000.

In this case, *rehabilitation* (what Dudek considers the provision of artificial limbs) is preferable to *maintenance* (the provision of a manual or power wheelchair) not only in terms of human values but in terms of minimizing costs. There can be several trade-offs for achieving a specific goal of life adaptation, where small increments of rehabilitation are equivalent to large increments of maintenance. But this requires use of rehabilitation. What if this person doesn't use his artificial limbs? Because such prostheses are often uncomfortable or even painful, what if he only wants to use them part of the time and use a wheelchair the rest of the time?

The rehabilitation of many individuals may not be as cost efficient as maintenance combined with environmental modifications. For example, equipping a hundred dual amputees with prosthetic limbs in a large metropolitan area may be less cost-efficient than providing them with wheelchairs and smoothly paved streets and buildings with ramps (which will also benefit people pushing carts and delivery persons with handtrucks). But when an environment cannot be easily or cost-efficiently modified, it may be less costly to rehabilitate and equip relatively few individuals.

Such models of costs and benefits say a lot about comparisons among numbers, but little about people. While they do have an important role, they should always be critically evaluated as far as why they were done, by whom, how well and for what purpose. Their value in providing a broad overview for budgeting and policy making should never come at the sacrifice of decisions regarding *individuals'* maintenance and rehabilitation.

Devices make possible negative as well as positive changes for people with disabilities. When recommending a device for a person's use, it is crucial to:

- assess a person's strengths as well as limitations,

- evaluate the existence of ancillary limitations (such as low vision for the user of an AAC system),

- select the most cost-efficient device that is the best ergonomic and aesthetic match,

- provide training in use and maintenance,

- and follow-up to determine the extent to which the device is meeting the consumer's needs and determine any secondary effects it may have presented.[2]

It is also important to keep in mind

a) the characteristics of the environment or milieu in which the device will be used,

b) the person's personality and preferences,

c) and the capabilities and characteristics of the technology under consideration.

The recommendation will thus emerge from that person's unique needs and will be consumer-driven.

Some tough, but important, questions that should be asked every individual considering the purchase or adoption of any assistive technology are:

1. What do you — not someone else — think you need?

2. What is it exactly that makes you think that? What's led you to that decision or opinion?

3. What is a typical day like for you — from the time you get up to the time you go to bed at night? Describe your activities, the people you usually see, the places you go.

4. What do you *wish* a typical day will be like one year from now? Five years and ten years from now?

5. What do you see as being most useful and helpful to you now? In the future in achieving your goals?

When the answers to these five questions suggest assistive technology use, then the next series of questions should ask:

6. What do you want to *do*?

7. Where? In what different environments or settings?

8. What assistance is already available in those settings? What will assistive technology use add to — or take away from — that assistance?

9. What changes in lifestyle are involved? For whom?

10. What non-technical solutions are available? What are their pros and cons?

11. What's the lowest level technical solution that will meet your needs and achieve the goal?

12. How well will it function in the various situations where you will use it?

Above all, realize that the purpose of an assistive technology is to enhance a person's functioning, esteem and quality of life. If the device doesn't do that, it will not be used. Nor, perhaps, should it.

Some important questions that should be asked of every consumer considering the use of any assistive technology are:

1. What do you — not someone else — think you need?
2. What is it exactly that makes you think that? What's led you to that decision or opinion? How much do you know about the device and its benefits? What does its use regularly require? Do you know anyone who is presently using it?
3. Please describe one of your typical days, from the time you get up to the time you go to bed at night, including your activities, the people you usually see, the places you go.
4. Describe what you *wish* a typical day will be like one year from now. Five years and ten years from now.
5. What do you see as being most useful and helpful to you now? In the future in achieving your goals?

When the answers to these five questions suggest assistive technology use, then the next series of questions should ask:

6. What do you want to do?
7. Where? In what different environments or settings?
8. What assistance is already available in those settings? What will assistive technology use add to — or take away from — that assistance?
9. What changes in lifestyle are involved? For whom?
10. What non-technical solutions are available? What are the pros and cons to them?
11. What's the lowest level technical solution that will meet your needs and achieve the goal?
12. How well is it functioning in the various situations where you use it?

Above all, realize that the purpose of an assistive technology is to enhance a person's functioning, esteem and quality of life. If the device doesn't do that, it will not be used. Nor, perhaps, should it.

SUMMARY

An organizing schema such as the **MPT Model** has considerable practical value. While rehabilitation engineering settings are very responsive to the physical needs of individuals with disabilities, there is frequently less attention given to the psychological and social aspects of assistive device use. By consulting a model such as the **MPT Model**,[3] the need for a potential intervention is flagged so that an initial profile suggesting non-use can be changed to one favoring use. This will reduce device abandonment, decrease premature or inappropriate device recommendations, and help assure that those individuals who can most benefit from a device will not only receive it, but will use it. Documentation of the initial and post-intervention profiles can:

a) help provide the rationale for funding a device or training for that device,

b) demonstrate an individual's improvement in functioning over time, and

c) help organize information typifying the needs of clientele.

REFERENCE NOTES

[1] Research on technology use is still in its infancy. One problem involves the use of methodologies that make inter study comparisons difficult. For example, two common approaches are:

a) population studies of device utilization rates where, after a certain amount of time has elapsed, people are grouped into user or non-user groups and their differentiating characteristics are analyzed, and

b) retrospective case studies where the focus is on individual characteristics that resulted in device use or non-use. Complicating matters further, the first approach typically employs objective measures of utilization whereas case studies are used in the second type which rely predominantly on subjective reports of individual characteristics. A combined approach of quantitative and qualitative assessment has been found to be useful (Scherer, 1986; Scherer & McKee, 1991). along with the following caveats when conducting consumer surveys:

1. Response rates may be low with the extremely satisfied, or the

very dissatisfied tend to respond more readily and frequently.

2. If consumers require the assistance of a family member or personal attendant to complete the survey, the responses will reflect *both* persons' point-of-view.

3. Even when taking into account the necessary modifications to ensure responses from persons with fine motor and sensory impairments, it will be too much work for some people *physically*.

Selected interviews with persons representing pre-specified categories of consumers, where responses can be probed in more depth, have a better track record of yielding useful as well as representative results.

Other methodological difficulties frequently encountered are studies that discuss the use of devices as an ancillary finding to another research question, such as functional independence. For example, Welch, Lobley, O'Sullivan, and Freed (1986) conducted a follow-up study of level C6 and C7 spinal cord injured individuals three months to four years post rehabilitation and presented results that indicated differential functional independence in self-care tasks. They provided data showing some dramatic declines in assistive device use from rehabilitation to follow-up. But because they had not made provision in their questionnaire to explore the reasons for device use or non-use, they could only say:

> A noticeable decrease in equipment used in dressing activities by both groups was probably related to the drop in skill levels in this area and increased personal care assistance. In other areas, it was not clear if equipment was discarded because it was no longer needed, or because it was too difficult or awkward to use once in the community (p. 239).

More problematic issues occur when researchers neglect or bypass the input of users and accept that offered by parents and other caretakers (e.g., DiCowden, 1990), fail to control for type and severity of disability (for example, including both paraplegics and quadriplegics in a study), and do not account for changes over time in the kinds of rehabilitation services and opportunities offered to persons who differ in age and number of years disabled (for example, include persons one year or less to 24 years or more post-rehabilitation). Also, there has been a remarkable increase in the availability and use of assistive technologies during the timespan of some studies.

[2]   In National Rehabilitation Hospital's "A Guide to Making Informed Choices about Assistive Technology" (Galvin, Ross, & Phillips, 1990), the following questions about key device characteristics are listed:

1.   Functional utility — what does it really do?

2.   The level of technology — how complicated is it? How hard is it to learn to use?

3.   Competition — Is the device similar to something they are already using?

4.   Clinical considerations — How is the device prescribed? Is a prescription necessary?

5.   Peer approval — Who is already using it? It's important for the device to function like it's supposed to AND to look acceptable.

6.   Formal evaluation — What sort of evaluation has the device seen? Has it been determined to be safe and reliable?

7.   Distribution — Where is it available? Is it stocked or does it have to be ordered?

8.   Maintenance — If the device has to be sent back to the factory for service, does the dealer rent or loan a substitute?

Schweitzer (1989) lists many questions to answer when planning to equip a person with an assistive device. Several are very similar to those listed above, but he adds the following:

1.   Will it truly enhance functioning or independence?

2.   How expensive is the system? Is there a less expensive device which performs comparatively? Does the life of the device seem justified for its cost?

3.   Is there a simpler solution?

4.   Does the system increase the client's dependence on a technical device without a backup solution in the event of equipment failure?

5.   Does the system interface well in the work or home environment? Is it compatible with other devices/systems the person is using?

A Collaborative Model for Matching Persons with Technologies

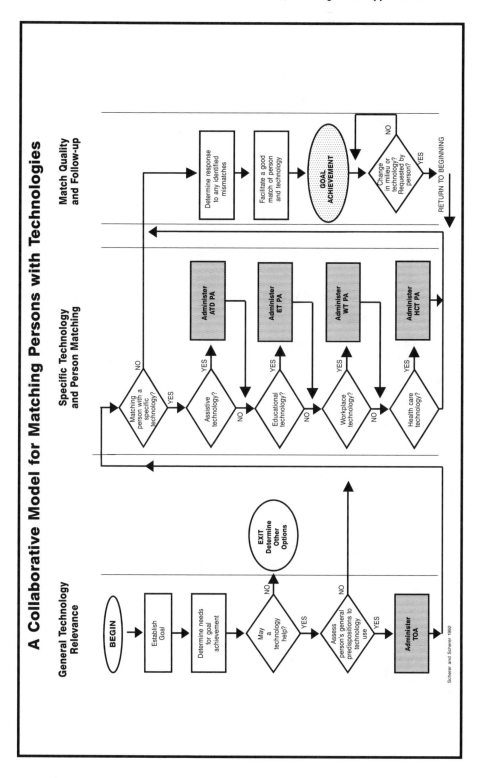

Scherer and Scherer 1992

Alexandra Enders (1984) also listed factors important to consider before prescribing or obtaining an assistive device:

1. Just whose life is being assisted and in what way?

2. Whose life is being made more work?

3. Whose needs are being addressed?

4. Who is the consumer?

5. Does the consumer want a change?

6. Does someone else want a change?

7. Is it worth the effort for the individual to use the device?

8. What options does the individual have if he or she doesn't use the device?

[3] Two assistive technology assessment/screening instruments were developed to assure that:

a) Consumer input would drive the **Matching Person and Technology (MPT)** process,

b) the degree of match between consumer and professional perspectives could be assessed,

c) professionals are guided into considering all relevant influences on device use while focusing primarily on the consumer's quality of life,

d) other professionals and consumers could verify the existence and importance of the influences on assistive technology use that emerged from this research, and

e) possible mismatches between a proposed technology and a potential user could be flagged in the hopes that early identification would reduce non-use or inappropriate use of assistive technologies and the disappointment and frustration that often accompanies less than ideal use.

The two assessment instruments are **The Assistive Technology Device Predisposition Assessment (ATD PA)** consumer and professional versions (Scherer & McKee, 1989), which are designed to be used as a set. An **Educational Technology Predisposition Assessment (ET PA)** (Scherer, McKee & Young, 1990), **Workplace Technol-**

ogy Predisposition Assessment (WT PA) (Scherer & McKee, 1991), **Health Care Technology Predisposition Assessment (HCT PA)** (Scherer, 1992) and **Technology Overload Assessment (TOA)** (Scherer & Weissberger, 1989) are also available. All instruments have a checklist format, are situational and were designed for consumer-driven matching of person and technology. The instruments are currently in pilot form and are undergoing further refinement as information concerning their usefulness is collected across the U.S. and abroad. Preliminary analyses indicate that they have good inter-rater reliability and criterion-related validity (since the items emerged from the actual experiences of users and non-users, they have content validity).

Section III:
Future Directions

CHAPTER EIGHT

Living in the State of Stuck

"Man is born free yet everywhere he is in chains."
Rousseau

Technology alone is rarely the answer to a person's enhanced quality of life. Assistive technologies can help a person access more opportunities and exercise more options, but they require support services and training, attention to the person's personality, preferences, and capabilities, and the characteristics of the milieu in which the device will be used. Rehabilitation professionals, whether counselors, physicians, nurses, engineers or occupational or physical therapists, must increase their focus on the psychosocial aspects of individuals' quality of life. There are just too many basic unmet needs that require attention before assistive technologies should even be considered.

One concern of such great importance that it requires special emphasis is the active involvement of the user in the decision-making process. Too often, individuals with disabilities are excluded from decisions regarding assistive technologies and other matters which affect their lives. This perpetuates the belief that persons with disabilities are passive and incompetent.

The involvement of consumers in the design and prototyping of assistive technologies would help assure that they result in safe and reliable functional gain, are comfortable to use and aesthetically pleasing, and that self-esteem and quality of life are enhanced by their use. As Chris advised,

> Utilize the pool of users to try out new equipment and for *their* input, which can be considerably positive at times as far as the contribution of ideas.

Most consumers realize the value of their involvment and many would be willing to participate in prototyping, as the following illustrate:

> Maggie: Disabled people should develop devices. I myself have suggestions for improvements if someone would just ask me.

Jim: I think they should ask users more often what they see the uses being, not just to assume they're going to be helpful.

Ken: There is a definite need for more prototyping. Let us have input into it because too many times we have stuff that's not appropriate.

Consumers are the ideal choice for prototyping assistive technologies. There are many technically oriented consumers with disabilities who, like Maggie, are just waiting to be asked for their opinions. Consumers (and parents of young consumers) are naturally motivated and their involvement should be encouraged.

In addition to the value of prototyping, all assistive technologies, especially the "non-essential" ones, might achieve higher utilization rates if more users were available as role models. According to Chris,

For those who are among device-using peers, the peer pressure will be an encouraging factor.

And from Ken's perspective,

Many people might find devices less imposing if a peer was used as a model — to get the person interested.

Peer modeling and support are valuable for presenting assistive technologies as options to individuals. Peer modelling is also helpful for the development of self-confidence and a positive identity and for learning adaptive behaviors in general.

ASSISTIVE DEVICES
AS KEYS TO MAINSTREAMING

Assistive devices are important enabling factors in mainstreaming and community integration and can potentially equalize the capabilites of persons with and without disabilities. They can render a disability irrelevant or, at least, relegate it to a minor role (Perlman & Austin, 1984). As Chris said,

Sure they equalize — from a distance! Now all students are using Macs and laser videodiscs, and none of them are having enough of that crucial human contact.

Chris' recent retirement has given her time to reflect back upon her own life and career and to stay in frequent contact with many of her former clients. Having grown up in institutions, Chris has had a longstanding interest in observing her clients, their relationships with technologies, and their mainstreamed experiences. She pointed out that in the past, young people in institutions had many more peer contacts than those in today's mainstreamed settings. She believes that mainstreaming can inhibit as much as stimulate a person's development.

> During my days of rehabilitation, the community had no services for me and others with polio. But in the hospital and rehabilitation institution, I had peers I could talk with, share things with. Today, if you're in an institution, you're with elderly persons and have few, if any, young peers.
>
> Mainstreaming is *hard*. The differences become so marked. And when you're a needle in the haystack, it's very hard to find other needles.
>
> Today, people with disabilities don't meet enough people within their abilities. We need to build peer groups around rehabilitation programs that then get absorbed into the community.

Chris is concerned that young people with disabilities do not have frequent opportunities, either inside or outside their mainstreamed educational settings, to talk with others similarly disabled in order to share ideas and experiences. Without such sharing, it is more difficult for them to establish a firm identity.

But, as Jim's example illustrates, mainstreaming does not necessarily prevent mutual sharing and contact with peers does not guarantee it. A 31-year-old woman with cerebral palsy, who spent many years in an institution with others similarly disabled, married a man with cerebral palsy (CP) and they are living independently. She highlighted the isolation of being institutionalized with peers when she said:

> Until a few months ago, I didn't know I had this [degenerative arthritis]. I thought every CP had this pain and that it was just a part of me, part of having CP. One night I asked my husband, 'What do you do about the pain you're having?' And he said, 'What pain?' I said, 'The pain we all have... don't you know what I mean?' He said, 'No.' And that's the first I was aware my pain was different.

In Chapter One Chuck said that his rehabilitation occurred in a social vacuum. In a later interview he said,

> We felt imprisoned. Whenever a quad [person with quadriplegia] came
> in for a checkup or something, we would ask what it's like on the outside.

The lack of access to appropriate peers is a major gap in the rehabilitation
system that people have tried to fill on their own through such enter-
prises as the establishment of wheelchair sports teams and fellowships
for the disabled. Computer networks and bulletin boards link individuals with shared interests and provide a wide array of information to
subscribers, but one must first have access to a computer. While these
options help provide some peer contact, the gaps can hardly be said to be
filled.

There are problems with mainstreaming, but the bottom line is that
it offers the best hope for the majority of young persons with disabilities
to participate in ordinary mainstream life in their community. Kate ad-
dresses the kind of social vacuum that can exist for individuals with
cerebral palsy who today live in a group home:

> You know, Marcia, I couldn't stand living in one of our residences. We
> are so over-regulating people's lives. They're always working on some
> goal or another and staff have to be constantly documenting it and
> writing it down. The residents are exhausted. They haven't been taught
> ways to handle free time because they have no free time. And they don't
> know how to plan their own day because it's planned for them. Now I
> can understand the staff viewpoint — you have to do things for effi-
> ciency when you have 10 residents and only two staff. But that's the same
> as what institutions do — work on efficiency rather than on individual
> needs.

As Chris said,

> It's not good to have disabled people only with others with the same
> disability. You can't win by keeping everyone in their own basket.

On this, she and Butch were in agreement. When I had asked Butch in
1991 if he had ever had any interest in joining a support group, he said:

> People really get tired of looking at other people in their shape. What's
> the fun of sitting around and talking to a bunch of people who know the
> exact something you know? Because they don't know any more, because
> they're not doing any more — and probably less.

While the individuals in this book acknowledged as many problems as benefits with mainstreaming, many advocated a combination of mainstreamed experiences and peer contact and support as an ideal solution to the weaknesses in each single approach. Ken summarized this perspective:

> I have a lot of problems with mainstreaming in general. I think it's left a lot of people isolated, but depending on the disability. A secondary support group on the side would allow for sharing of feelings and experiences. I think people would be isolated more if they weren't mainstreamed and stayed alone in their own little group. They could be content but may get an institutionalized mentality. Without mainstreaming it's a lot harder to face the outside world. Rather than full, people should consider partial mainstreaming.

Some persons with cerebral palsy said that they believe the combination of mainstreaming and peer contact would have greatly enhanced their own (re)socialization efforts. For example, one woman said,

> If I had been mainstreamed as a child, I'd be better adjusted and have more self-confidence now.

Yet, people in mainstreamed settings are often expected to be "normal" while, at the same time, they are not treated "normally." They face dilemmas such as being told, "You're just like everyone else, but you need different programs and equipment." Such mixed messages can lead to confusion and distress.

90% of Physical Rehabilitation is Mental Rehabilitation

Several people in this book wished they had received counseling to improve their self-image and self-confidence. According to Butch, there needs to be a heightened emphasis on the psychological aspects of rehabilitation. He explained,

> People in this condition need mental rehabilitation more than anything else. Because that is 90% of physical rehabilitation. [Rehabilitation doesn't] want to face that because it's too expensive. So you adapt. You develop coping mechanisms and some of them, like drinking, are not good ones. If way back then they had given us good coping mechanisms,

a lot of problems could have been prevented.

Early on, when you're totally receptive to learning something and your mind wants to find out what all the ands, ifs, and buts are about, if they would get your inhibitions out, have a psychotherapist come in to get you talking, get you adjusted to the *thought* of it. But once you get four or so years down the road, you're totally in a rut, stuck. If I'd been given a chance to hash out what was going on in my mind, things probably would've been a whole lot different for me.

This is very similar to Chuck's point in Chapter One:

I wish I'd had counseling regularly... on a fairly regular basis. I'm not sure what would've come out of it, but if you see someone enough, eventually you're going to say something. Try to bring things out, some of the anger, and things like that. That was something that was never done, and that anger just sits in there and grows.

A person with a recent spinal cord injury said,

In rehab they handle your broken neck, but the broken neck isn't the problem. The paralysis is the problem. They don't confront the paralysis.

And Jim lamented that:

I know I do good work and get the job done like "normal" people, but yet I realize I'm different, that I'm handicapped. And it's frustrating, because I have devices and... I've had a lot of rehabilitation but not much counseling and we need more counseling to go with the devices.

When I asked Ken, the counselor with a spinal cord injury, what he thought about the need for counseling services in rehabilitation, he said:

Right now the emphasis is on getting people up to the highest level they can physically. They don't have the time right now to help people bring up their self-esteem. I think somewhere down the line, they may have to work on it. It's going to have to be mainly on an outpatient basis — they'll have to start the person as an inpatient, and then follow the person. Rehab will get better. It's continuously gotten better through the years and will continue to do so. I think the same thing with assistive devices. The only thing is, I hope they don't get so good that a ... well... what I'm thinking of is a vendor may spend a lot of money to block research and rehab, so that their equipment is always needed. Anyway, the focus of rehab should be on getting people to do as much as they can, and even more, on the person's sense of self-worth.

Counseling services need to be (re)incorporated into comprehensive rehabilitation programs. Individuals would like opportunities to discuss and work through feelings, attitudes, and fears that interfere with rehabilitation. Counseling specialists, trained to have an interactive, comprehensive and interdisciplinary approach to problem intervention can, as Chris said, "Look at the whole picture: pride, motivation, confidence, coping, one's outlook on life — all those elusive things." They can help people resolve identity confusion and come to terms with and enhance their own unique circumstances. For some persons, this may mean developing a positive view of their differences. As Garris (1983) said:

> I mentally cringe when I hear disabled persons say they are like everyone else — I am not and I know why. My life experiences have been quite different, the problems that I've had to solve have been different. It's little wonder that I'm different in so many ways. Viva.

Finally, counselors can educate and provide support to rehabilitation agencies and other members of the rehabilitation team. While educated for technical careers, engineers increasingly find themselves in the position of needing to provide more human services and psychosocial interventions. These highly motivated and relatively new additions to the comprehensive rehabilitation team merit increased attention to their unique roles.

In Search of the Human Touch

Sociologist Irving Zola points out, through examples of his own experiences with a disability, that no one, with or without a disability, is *truly* "independent." Rather than having independence as the goal of rehabilitation, it is better to provide individuals with the skills to:

- exercise self-directed choices,
- manage their feelings,
- request assistance with dignity and refuse it with diplomacy,
- and learn to be assertive in job maintenance and advancement and in the establishment of new relationships.

Then, individuals can ask for help without feeling they've lost self-control, individuality or independence and can better choose to use or not use devices.

Zola views technological assistance as the exchange of one dependency (human beings) for another (assistive devices). Regarding the use of devices, he asks: "Where does a healthy pursuit of independence end and a sad withering of human contact begin?" He cautions against objectifying care into a technical service, thereby objectifying the individuals receiving that service. He believes even "patronizing or infantilizing" care is preferable to assistance from robots or specially trained monkeys because, as unacceptable or undesirable as these are, they are at least human qualities.

Brian, too, expressed in Chapter Five why he believes robotics and monkeys are not the answer for people with disabilities. He used the example of feeding and said that some of his best times involved the close interactions that occurred then. For many persons like Brian, life without assistance is not an option. Yet, people cannot be blithely given a machine; people want and need people, interpersonal interaction and warmth.

There are positive and negative aspects to both assistive device use and the use of personal assistance. While personal assistance is said to be the "key to employability of persons with physical disabilities" (Nosek, 1990), there are many cases where personal attendants have exploited consumers through theft or physical abuse (Ulicny, White, Bradford, & Mathews, 1990). Numerous examples were given in Chapter Seven of the benefits and pitfalls of assistive device use. The best course of action seems to be the prudent selection of the best of each. As Zola has stated, "It's not the quality of tasks we can perform without assistance, but the quality of life we can live with help... (p. 123)." Interdependence over independence.

Brian, 1991

In August, I was in San Francisco for a conference and had called Brian to see if it was possible for us to get together. He lived about sixty miles away, but offered to drive to the nearest station and then "BART in" to meet me.

I recognized him in the crowd instantly. He was leaning over reading a book and was wearing a tie-dyed shirt, pea jacket, necklace and jeans.

His hair was even longer now, and he wore it tied back in a pony tail. He was just as thin and lanky as ever.

The first thing he shared with me was a recent experience he had of standing up (he was held in a vertical position by straps). I asked what it was like after ten years.

"Like seeing the ocean for the first time, it was that great."

Then Brian announced that he is going back to school to study computer animation. This in addition to his three jobs: ushering at a local theater, continuing to tutor students in math, and visiting schools and teaching young people "about what people with disabilities are really like."

Brian's example underscores the value of a combination of personal and technical assistance. As he describes, such combined support has enabled him to live as active a life as anyone.

> I still only need personal assistance for getting in and out of bed and doing chores around the house. I hire a few good people to come in at certain times of the day to help. With this, I'm able to get the best quality care I need.
>
> My two legs and two motorcycle wheels have turned into a four wheel motorized chair. That chair is now my freedom and independence. And, here I am, living life to its fullest.

After he arrived in California, he pursued his recreational interests "with a vengeance." In July, 1989, he received a certificate in sailing and a year later one in scuba diving. He has tried para-sailing, surfing, and has gone white-water rafting. He continues his interest in sit-skiing and kayaking. Most recently, he had a "bungee jumping experience" from a hot air balloon:

> Two tether ropes were hooked to the basket so it would reach one height and stop. Three people could fit at one time. The first jumper got in and the balloon went up to 150 feet. The jumper squatted on the rim of the basket and leapt off as if he were doing a swan dive into a pool. He did a freefall until he got to the end of the bungee cord, which caused him to stop 100 feet later, and then up he went again 50 feet and so on like something on a rubber band. A few minutes later he came to a stop and the pilot lowered the balloon to where a team of people were there to catch him.
>
> Forty people jumped that day, and not one chickened out. I heard them say, 'It was the scariest thing I've ever done' and 'It was the closest

thing to death I've ever felt—you've got to do it!' Well, after hearing that, I had to do it. I wore a harness around my shoulders and hips and my legs were strapped together. The director of the trip held me in a honeymoon carry. Then we went up to 150 feet and, before I had time to think what I was really doing up there, we left the balloon.

It's hard to describe that feeling of falling. I'm glad I did it but I don't think I'll do it again. Still, after that experience I feel like I can do anything.

You know, after my accident I kept a journal of events that evolved each day, positive or negative. Reading them now, thirteen years later, the growth I see is mind boggling. I owe my parents so much thanks. They played a big part in getting my feet back on the ground — so to speak!

While Brian is living an *active* life, he is still waiting for the intimate relationship he wants to have a *complete* life.

I do look forward to a married life at some point. I still haven't found the right girl, but I have had several close girlfriend relationships. It takes time and understanding and, most of all, communication. My heart seems to speak first, and then my head follows. I don't know. . . there's always some hidden expectation and somebody ends up getting hurt. But without love in a dream, it'll never come true.

A few months passed, and then I received a letter from Brian. He started out talking about the 1991 Berkeley and Oakland fires and then, almost as a postscript, he wrote,

Oh yeah, I ended up in the hospital for five days with pneumonia and a collapsed lung. The flu hit hard here and I was a victim. No sleep for three days and my lungs felt like they were filled with a gallon of fluid. In comparison, it feels like the wind getting knocked out of you. It brought back a lot of old memories and made me realize *again* how lucky I am to be alive. Perhaps this will become a new chapter, or my third life. Who knows... what a strange trip it's been.

For the past week it's been sunny and 75 degrees. My new parrot and I just got back from a walk to the beach. She's getting to be a real ham on our trips. She has a funny whistle and loves to be held by the people that stop and talk with us — especially the ones with ear rings.

[Always, Brian]

In March, Brian's stamina and resilience were put to the test again. While driving on Highway 1, his parrot was having some difficulty which caused Brian to glance at and reach toward her. He "lost control of the van and went into a bridge. I broke my leg, three ribs, and I have a punctured lung."

He is currently recuperating.

Part of "living life to the fullest" for Brian is being able to take as many risks as a person without a disability. While the consequences he endures from his bout with pneumonia and the injuries from his accident in his van have resulted in complications a non-disabled person would not have, this is much more preferable to him than the inability to exercise choice and take risks.

"One May Learn to Ambulate on Artificial Limbs, But Have Nowhere to Walk"

In the late sixties, in Great Society times, an essay was written on "Professional Antitherapy" (Kutner, 1969) that said, in part:

> [Patients are expected to play a passive-receptive role throughout their rehabilitation]. On the one hand, the patient is taught how to get well again by means of specific techniques of muscle and habit training. On the other hand, this education is carried out in a social vacuum, divorced from the hurly-burly of daily life. The patient is taught generically useful habits but is kept from exercising them by a contrived context not remotely approaching the vicissitudes of life in open society. One may learn to ambulate on artificial limbs, but have nowhere to walk; ... learn to speak, but have no one to communicate with or no drive to use this power to gain useful objectives (e.g. negotiating for a new apartment, arranging for transportation, joining a club or church, developing new friends) (pp. 177-8).

While the above appeared 24 years ago, the individuals who have shared their experiences in this book have all showed that it is still quite current. Several said that, in spite of such efforts as the UN Decade of Disabled Persons (which ended in 1992), the Americans with Disabilities Act and their own accomplishments, they still feel inadequate, like marginal participants in society. They feel abandoned or betrayed by the system designed to help them.

Too many persons with disabilities in the U.S. are going into the 21st century with what Ken termed "a low grade depression". They are angry, anxious, and alienated. For some, old friends have disappeared without new ones to take their place or there has been a deliberate rejection of friends. Like Butch in the early years after his injury, they feel connected to no one, find hope in nothing. They often have become emotionally inhibited or repressed. They are lonely and they believe that no one understands their feelings — or cares. Goals, potential, purpose, meaning are elusive. They are in cycles of despair and many eventually commit suicide.

Though some individuals will cope by withdrawing, or turning to alcohol and drug abuse, or developing chronic health problems, others will cope through a "drive to survive," and have their sights set on opportunities, not limitations. Just how any given individual's *disabled experience* comes to be characterized depends on the complex mix of details comprising the person's temperament, expectations, prior experiences and opportunities, and psychosocial environment. It also depends on aspects of the disability and the type and amount of rehabilitation and *empowering resources* made available to the person, (for example, assistive devices and vocational training).

Butch said in 1991 that:

> We need to change our own attitudes and those of society — have people and society better blend, them to us and us to them.

The quality of life a person with a disability is able to achieve is interactive and contextual. It is affected by the rehabilitation system's emphasis on its own maintenance rather than the provision of full and comprehensive rehabilitation. It is a direct derivative of the importance placed on the modification of individual deficits, the message to be compliant yet independent, to be yourself yet to emulate the "ideal," to see assistive devices as keys to new opportunities, but to keep expectations realistic. It is very much influenced by on-again, off-again legislation and society's degree of tolerance at any given moment. It is tremendously impacted by the subtle message that machines and technology will provide a better life.

We are *physically* rehabilitating people — far beyond what has ever been possible before now. But we are rehabilitating people into what? We need to keep asking that question until we can come to define *rehabilitation success* primarily in terms of quality of life, and not in defense of the quality of care or quality of technology that has been provided.

THE LIFE STORIES OF PEOPLE WITH DISABILITIES ARE METAPHORS FOR EVERYONE

When personal computers flooded the country in the 1980's they fueled dreams of possibility and freedom from the more mundane aspects of life. Their widespread use has often isolated people and created highly pitched and stressful work environments as we increasingly work in a truly global village.

By many accounts, technological advances have not made us happier or our world better. We remain a society modeled after the machine where conformity, synchrony and predictability reign.

So it seems, **we are stuck**. We live in a society with many opportunities, but we increasingly have fewer freedoms within them. We are all confused by social advances and retreats and sophisticated medical and technical achievements that have made us feel as if we're merely entities composed of machine replaceable parts. Now that our jobs can be done by computers, our hearts kept going by pacemakers, our unhealthy organs replaced by those taken from someone else, we find ourselves wondering if we really need more and better technical advances. There is no cure for AIDS, our air is badly polluted, and old diseases like cholera and tuberculosis are fast becoming daily topics of conversation. All is not running as smoothly as the machine. Yet we have become less interdependent on people and more dependent on technology. And technology is letting us down.

Chris had said during one of our conversations,

> If they want to make saving lives an important thing, then they have to employ the resources to make those lives worthwhile.

Now we are thinking that we need, as Ken said in Chapter Five, improvement first in the *basic* things like quality education, affordable health care and housing.

Quality of life is not just the absence of poverty, pain, and other aspects of human suffering. It is not just extending the length of the lifespan. It isn't about the prevention of dying, but the enhancement of living. It is not a matter for only social scientists and health care professionals. Quality of life is the sum total of the way we feel and think about ourselves, the environments we put ourselves into, the kinds of people we associate with, the systems and institutions with which we choose to become involved, the goals we have, the opportunities we are able to pursue, and the belief we have in our potential to effectively act on our environment. It is having purpose and meaning and having a "vital connection" to the world around us. While technology does provide many people with an important means of "connecting," it is only one means.

No one wants technology to be taken away. But its use should come from choice, not from having it be hurled unrelentlessly on us. We need to understand both how technology has impacted society and how our own social priorities and contexts have shaped the emergence of particular technologies — and how we want this to be played out in the future.

For too many of us, our potential has gone unrealized, promises to us have gone unfulfilled. We're encouraged to be individuals, but pushed to do as we're told. We frequently feel alienated from family, friends, and the systems designed to support and help us. We can speak but often have no one to talk with. We're unsure of our purpose, what the future holds. The old order is crumbling everywhere and there is a pervasive "lowgrade depression" and sense of despair. We feel out of control, that we're caught between having it all and not having much of anything, that we're **living in the state of stuck**. Through it all, the machines and the computers keep rolling along. Yet, if we think we "ain't got nothing to fight with, then you lose your will."

References

Alexander, J.L. & Willems, E.P. (1981). Quality of life: Some measurement requirements. *Archives of Physical Medicine & Rehabilitation*, 62, 261-265.

Altheide, MR, Scarborough, WB, & Mitchell, DA. (1990). Computer use at home and work by developmentally delayed adults. In H. Murphy (Ed.), *Proceedings of the Fifth Annual Conference, "Technology and Persons with Disabilities"* (pp. 11-22). Los Angeles: Office of Disabled Student Services, California State University, Northridge.

Anderson, T.P. (1982). Quality of life and the individual with a disability. *Archives of Physical Medicine and Rehabilitation, 63*, 55.

Andreasen, N.J.C. & Norris, A. (1972). Long-term adjustment and adaptation mechanisms in severely burned adults. *Journal of Nervous and Mental Disorders, 154*(5), 352.

Baskin, B.H. & Harris, K.H. (1984). *More Notes from a Different Drummer: A Guide to Juvenile Fiction Portraying the Disabled.* New York: Bowker.

Batavia, AI, Dillard, D, & Phillips, B. (1990). How to avoid technology abandonment. In H. Murphy (Ed.), *Proceedings of the Fifth Annual Conference, "Technology and Persons with Disabilities"* (pp.55-64). Los Angeles: Office of Disabled Student Services, California State University, Northridge.

Baum, D. D. (1982). *The human side of exceptionality.* Baltimore: University Park Press.

Baumeister, R.F. & Scher, S.J. (1988). Self-defeating behavior patterns among normal individuals: Review and analysis of common self-destructive tendencies. *Psychological Bulletin, 104*(1), 3-22.

Beniger, J.R. (1986). *The control revolution: Technological and economic origins of the information society.* Cambridge, MA: Harvard University Press.

Bennet, J. (April 12, 1992). Wave of sympathy for canine victim. *The New York Times.*

Benshoff, J.J., Janikowski, T.P., Taricone, P.F., & Brenner, J.S. (1990). Alcohol and drug abuse: A content analysis of the rehabilitation literature. *Journal of Applied Rehabilitation Counseling, 21*(4), 9-12.

Bermann, E. (1973). *Scapegoat: the impact of death-fear on an American family.* Ann Arbor: University of Michigan Press.

Bjorck-Akesson, E. (1990, August). Communicative interaction of young non-speaking children and their parents. Paper presented at The Fourth Biennial International ISAAC Conference on Augmentative and Alternative Communication, Stockholm, Sweden.

Blau, T.H. (1977). Quality of life, social indicators, and predictors of change. *Professional Psychology, 8,* 464-473.

Borysenko, J. (1987). *Minding the body, mending the mind.* Reading, Mass.: Addison-Wesley.

Bowe, F.G. (1984). *Personal computers and special needs.* Berkeley, CA: Sybex.

Bowe, F.G. (1988/Aug./Sept.). Why seniors don't use technology. *Technology Review, 91,* 33-40.

Braun, S. (1987, Summer). Psycho-neurooooo-what? *Rochester Review* (Alumni Magazine of the University of Rochester School of Medicine and Dentistry).

Brooks, N, & Hoyer, E. (1989). Consumer evaluation of assistive devices. In J. Presperin (Ed.), *Proceedings of the RESNA 12th Annual Conference: Technology for the Next Decade* (pp. 358-359). Washington, DC: RESNA Press.

Brooks, N, & Redden, M.R. (1986). Scientists and engineers with disabilities evaluate assistive devices. *Proceedings of the RESNA 9th Annual Conference* (pp. 1-2). Washington, DC: RESNA.

Campbell, A. (1976). Subjective measures of well-being. *American Psychologist, 3,* 117-124.

Cassell, E. (1991). Recognizing suffering. *The Hastings Center Report, 21*(3), 24.

Children's Hospital at Stanford. (1980). *Team effectiveness: A retrospective study.* Palo Alto, California: Rehabilitation Engineering Center. (NARIC document No. 03855).

Chubon, R.A. (1985). Quality of life measurement of persons with back problems: Some preliminary findings. *Journal of Applied Rehabilitation Counseling, 16*(2), 31- 34.

Coelho, R.J. & Dillon, N.F. (1990). A survey of elderly persons with developmental disabilities. *Journal of Applied Rehabilitation Counseling, 21*(1), 9-15.

Coelho, G., Hamburg, D., & Adams, J. (Eds.). (1974). *Coping and adaptation.* New York: Basic Books.

Collier, B., Norris, L., & Rothschild, N. (1990, August). Technology: What's working, what's not and why? Paper presented at The Fourth Biennial International ISAAC Conference on Augmentative and Alternative Communication, Stockholm, Sweden.

Condeluci, A. (1989). Empowering people with cerebral palsy. *Journal of Rehabilitation, 55*(2), 15-16.

Cousins, N. (1979). *Anatomy of an illness as perceived by the patient.* New York: Norton.

Cousins, N. (1984). *The healing heart.* New York: Avon Books.

Creech, R. (1990, August). Practical augmentative and alternative communication: The ultimate goal. Paper presented at The

Fourth Biennial International ISAAC Conference on Augmentative and Alternative Communication, Stockholm, Sweden.

Crewe, N. M. & Athelstan, G. T. (1984). *Functional assessment inventory manual.* Menomonie, WI: Materials Development Center, University of Wisconsin-Stout.

DiCowden, M. (1990). Pediatric rehabilitation: Special patients, special needs. *Journal of Rehabilitation*, 56(3), 13-17.

Dragona, J.J. (1985/2). The joys of advocacy: Will we ever be permitted to rest upon our laurels? *Disabled USA*, 34-35.

Dudek, R.A. (1982). *Human rehabilitation techniques: A technology assessment.* Paper presented at the national meeting of the American Hospital Association, New Orleans. (NARIC Document No. R002672).

Efthimiou, J., Gordon, W.A., Sell, H., & Stratford, C. (1981). Electronic assistive devices: Their impact on the quality of life of high level quadriplegic persons. *Archives of Physical Medicine & Rehabilitation*, 62, 131-134.

Enders, A. (1984). Questionable devices. *Proceedings of the Second Annual Meeting of the Rehabilitation Engineering Society of North America* (pp. 271-276). Bethesda, MD: Rehabilitation Engineering Society of North America (RESNA).

Erikson, E. (1963). *Childhood & society* (2nd Edition). New York: Norton.

Evans, R.W., Manninen, D.L., Garrison, L.P., Hart, L.G., Blagg, C.R., Gutman, R.A., Hull, A.R., & Lowrie, E.G. (1985). The quality of life of patients with end-stage renal disease. *New England Journal of Medicine*, 312(9), 553-559.

Fabian, E.S. (1991). Using quality-of-life indicators in rehabilitation program evaluation. *Rehabilitation Counseling Bulletin*. 34(4), 344-356.

Feit, S., Dutton, D., & DeKoff, M. (1990). Software for elementary children with mental retardation. In H. Murphy (Ed.), *Proceedings of the Fifth Annual Conference, "Technology and Persons with Disabilities"* (pp. 223-234). Los Angeles: Office of Disabled Student Services, California State University, Northridge.

Fenderson, D.A. (1984). Hightech/high touch: Making good on the promise. In Perlman & Austin (Eds.). *Technology and Rehabilitation of Disabled Persons in the Information Age*, a Report of the Eighth Mary E. Switzer Memorial Seminar, May, 1984. Washington, DC: National Rehabilitation Association.

Ferrier, L.J. (1990, August). A procedure for evaluating intelligibility of synthetic speech versus voice. Paper presented at The Fourth Biennial International ISAAC Conference on Augmentative and Alternative Communication, Stockholm, Sweden.

Flanagan, J.C. (1982). Measurement of quality of life: Current state of the art. *Archives of Physical Medicine and Rehabilitation*, 63, 56-59.

Frank, R.G., Wonderlich, S.A., Corcoran, J.R., Ashkanazi, G.S., & Wilson, R. (1984). Interpersonal response to spinal cord injury. Paper presented at the 92nd annual convention of the American Psychological Association, Los Angeles.

Franklin, B. (1990, August). The use of personal FM systems with hearing impaired preschoolers. Paper presented at The Fourth Biennial International ISAAC Conference on Augmentative and Alternative Communication, Stockholm, Sweden.

Frieden, L. (1980). Independent living models. *Rehabilitation Literature*, 41, 7-8.

Friedman, H.S. (1991). *The self-healing personality: Why some people achieve health and others succumb to illness*. New York: Henry Holt.

Gage, N.L. & Berliner, D.C. (1992). *Educational Psychology, Fifth Edition*. Boston: Houghton Mifflin.

Galvin, J, Ross, D, & Phillips, B. (1990). Meeting user needs through assistive technology. In H. Murphy (Ed.), *Proceedings of the Fifth Annual Conference, "Technology and Persons with Disabilities"* (pp. 269-278). Los Angeles: Office of Disabled Student Services, California State University, Northridge.

Garris, A.G. (1983/3). Is it righteous or outrageous: Responses to thoughts on rage and disability. *Disabled USA*, 10.

Gibson, N, Reid, B, & McCartney, N. (1990, August). Assessment in augmentative and alternative communication: Encompassing educational theory and practice. Paper presented at The Fourth Biennial International ISAAC Conference on Augmentative and Alternative Communication, Stockholm, Sweden.

Graves, W.H. (1991). Participatory action research: A new paradigm for disability and rehabilitation research. *ARCA News*, 19(1), 8-10.

Greer, B.G. (1986). Substance abuse among people with disabilities: A problem of too much accessibility. *Journal of Rehabilitation*, 52(1), 34-38.

Hansell, N. (1974). *The person-in-distress: On the biosocial mechanisms of adaptation*. New York: Behavioral Sciences Press.

Harris, L. & Associates. (1991). *Public attitudes toward people with disabilities*. National Council on disability. Washington, DC.

Hawkins, DB. (1984). Comparisons of speech recognition in noise by mildly-to-moderately hearing-impaired children using hearing aids and FM systems. *Journal of Speech and Hearing Disorders, 49*, 409-418.

Heinemann, A.W. (1991). Substance abuse and spinal cord injury. *Paraplegia News, 45*(7), 16.

Holland, B.E. & Falvo, D.R. (1990). Forgotten: Elderly persons with disability — a consequence of policy. *Journal of Rehabilitation, 56*(2), 32-35.

Humphry, D. (1991). *Final Exit*. Eugene, Oregon: The Hemlock Society.

Institute of Medicine (U.S.), Committee on a National Agenda for the Prevention of Disabilities. (1991). A.M. Pope & A.R. Tarlov (Eds.), *Disability in America: Toward a National Agenda for Prevention*. Washington, D.C.: National Academy Press.

International Center for the Disabled. (1986). *The ICD survey of disabled Americans: Bringing disabled Americans into the mainstream*. New York: Author.

Jeffrey, D.L. (1986). Hazards of reduced mobility for the person with a spinal cord injury. *Journal of Rehabilitation*. *52*(2), 59-62.

Kanigel, R. (April, 1986). Computers will help — someday. *Johns Hopkins Magazine*, 38-44.

Kaplan, S. & Questad, K. (1980). Client characteristics in rehabilitation studies: A literature review. *Journal of Applied Rehabilitation Counseling*, 11(4), 165-168.

Katz, Michael B. (1968) *The Irony of Early School Reform: Educational Innovation in Mid-Nineteenth Century Massachusetts*. Boston, MA: Beacon Press.

Katz, S. (Ed). (1987). The Portugal conference: Measuring quality of life and functional status in clinical and epidemiological research. *Journal of Chronic Disease*, Special Issue, *40*,(6), 459-650.

Kessler, D. (1986). All products are crutches: And lever door handles are easier for everybody. *Disabled USA*, 1-2.

Kottke, F.J. (1982). Philosophic considerations of quality of life for the disabled. *Archives of Physical Medicine and Rehabilitation*, 63, 60-62.

Kottke, F.J., Stillwell, G.K., & Lehmann, J.F. (1982). *Krusen's Handbook of Physical Medicine and Rehabilitation*. Philadelphia: W.B. Saunders Co.

Krause, J.S. (1992). Life satisfaction after spinal cord injury: A descriptive study. *Rehabilitation Psychology*, 37(1), 61-70

Krause, J.S. & Crewe, N.M. (1987). Prediction of long-term survival among persons with spinal cord injury: An 11-year prospective study. *Rehabilitation Psychology*, 32, 205-213.

Krause, J.S. & Dawis, R.V. (1992). Prediction of life satisfaction after spinal cord injury: A four-year longitudinal approach. *Rehabilitation Psychology*, 37(1), 49-60.

Kubler-Ross, E. (1969). *On death and dying*. New York: Macmillan.

Kutner, B. (1969). Professional antitherapy. *Journal of Rehabilitation*, 35(6), 16-18.

Laing, R.D. (1965). *Sanity, madness, and the family*. New York: Basic Books.

Laing, R.D. (1971). *The politics of the family and other essays*. New York: Pantheon Books.

Lassiter, R.A. (1972). History of the Rehabilitation Movement in America. In Cull, J.G. & Hardy, R.E. (Eds.). *Vocational Rehabilitation: Profession and Process*. Springfield, IL: Charles C. Thomas.

Lazarus, R.S., Averill, J.R., & Opton, E.M., Jr. (1974). The psychology of coping: Issues of research and assessment. In G.V. Coelho, D.A. Hamburg, & J.E. Adams (Eds.), *Coping and adaptation*. New York: Basic Books.

Lazarus, R.S. & Folkman, S. (1984). *Stress, appraisal, and coping*. New York: Springer Publishing Co.

Littrell, J.L. (1991). Women with disabilities in community college computer training programs. In H. Murphy (Ed.), *Proceedings of the Sixth Annual Conference, Technology and Persons with Disabilities* (pp. 553-562), California State University, Northridge.

Manicas, P.T., & Secord, P.F. (1983). Implications for psychology of the new philosophy of science. *American Psychologist, 38*(4), 399-413.

Matte, K.B., Crisler, J.R., Campbell, L., & Woodruff, C. (1991). Clients' functioning level as perceived by clients and rehabilitation professionals. *Journal of Applied Rehabilitation Counseling, 22*(2), 3-6.

Maynard, F.M. & Muth, A.S. (1987). The choice to end life as a ventilator-dependent quadriplegic. *Archives of Physical Medicine & Rehabilitation, 68*(12), 862-864.

McGrath, P.J., Goodman, J.T., Cunningham, S.J., MacDonald, B.J., Nichols, T.A., & Unruh, A. (1985). Assistive devices: Utilization by children. *Archives of Physical Medicine & Rehabilitation, 67*, 235-240.

Mitcham, C. & Grote, J. (1978). Philosophy of technology. In W.T. Reich (Ed.), *Encyclopedia of Bioethics* (pp. 829-840). New York: The Free Press.

Musselwhite, CR. (1990, August). Topic setting: Generic and specific strategies. Paper presented at The Fourth Biennial International ISAAC Conference on Augmentative and Alternative Communication, Stockholm, Sweden.

New York State Senate Select Committee on the Disabled, L. Paul Kehoe, Chairman. (1989). Coming to terms with disabilities: A compilation of vocabulary relating to visible and non-visible disabilities. Albany, New York: Author.

Nolan, C. (1987). *Under the eye of the clock: The life story of Christoper Nolan*. New York: St. Martin's Press.

Nosek, M.A. (1990). Personal assistance: Key to employability of persons with physical disabilities. *Journal of Applied Rehabilitation Counseling, 21*(4), 3-8.

Obermann, E.C. (1965). *A history of vocational rehabilitation in America.* Minneapolis: T.S. Denison & Co.

O'Brien, T. & DeLongis, A. (1991). A three-function model of coping: Emotion-focused, problem-focused, and relationship-focused. Paper presented at the 99th annual convention of the American Psychological Association, San Francisco.

Parsons, T. (1951). *The social system.* New York: The Free Press of Glencoe.

Perlman, L.G. & Austin, G.F. (1984). *Technology and rehabilitation of disabled persons in the information age.* A report of the Mary E. Switzer Memorial Seminar, May,1984. Washington, D.C.: National Rehabilitation Association.

Perlman, L.G. & Hansen, C.E. (Eds). (1989). *Technology and employment of persons with disabilities: A report on the 13th Mary E. Switzer memorial seminar.* Alexandria, Virginia: National Rehabilitation Association.

Pickering, GL, & Bristow, DC. (1990, August). *The impact of functional visual deficits in augmentative communication.* Paper presented at The Fourth Biennial International ISAAC Conference on Augmentative and Alternative Communication, Stockholm, Sweden.

Pitts, J.H. (1980). Predictors of rehabilitation success and failure of a caseload of hearing impaired clients. *Journal of Applied Rehabilitation Counseling*, 11(4), 200-202.

President's Committee on the Employment of People with Disabilities. (1984, January). Controversy over how technology best accommodates the disabled. *Newsletter for Industry*, pp. 1-4.

Rahimi, M.A. (1981/January). Intelligent prosthetic devices. *Computer*, p. 22.

Read, RF. (1990). Client evaluation and equipment prescription. In H. Murphy (Ed.), *Proceedings of the Fifth Annual Conference, "Technol-*

ogy and Persons with Disabilities" (pp. 553-564). Los Angeles: Office of Disabled Student Services, California State University, Northridge.

Redden, M. & Stern, V. (Eds). (1983). *Technology for independent living II.* Washington, DC: American Association for the Advancement of Science.

Reich, W.T. (1978). Quality of life. In W.T. Reich (Ed.), *Encyclopedia of Bioethics* (pp. 829-840). New York: The Free Press.

Roessler, R.T. (1990). A quality of life perspective on rehabilitation counseling. *Rehabilitation Counseling Bulletin*, 34(2), 82-90.

Rohe, D.E. & DePompolo. R.W. (1985). Substance abuse policies in rehabilitation medicine departments. *Archives of Physical Medicine & Rehabilitation*, 66, 701-703.

Rohe, D.E. & Krause, J.S. (1992, August). Stability of interests after severe physical disability: An 11-year longitudinal study. Paper presented at the 100th Annual Meeting of the American Psychological Association, Washington, D.C.

Root, A.A. (1970). What instructors say to the students makes a difference. *Engineering Education*, 61, 722-725.

Rosen, S.L. (1983). Learning to be handicapped. *Disabled USA*, (1), 7-9.

Rush, W.L. (1985). Not a fifth wheel: Sexual expression needs to be mainstreamed, too. *Disabled USA*, 2, 26-29.

Sacks, O. (1987). *Awakenings*. New York: Summit.

Scheer, L. (1980). Experience with quality of life comparisons. In A. Szalai & F.M. Andrews (Eds.). *The quality of life: Comparative studies* (pp. 146-155), Beverly Hills, CA: Sage Publications, Inc.

Scherer, M.J. (1992). *The Health Care Technology Predisposition Assessment (HCT PA)*. Rochester, NY.

Scherer, M.J. (1991a). Technology and mainstreamed students with physical disabilities: Perspectives toward the end of the 20th century. In M. Foster (Ed.), *Readings on Equal Education*, 11. New York: AMS Press.

Scherer, M.J. (1991b). Assistive technology use, avoidance and abandonment: What we know so far. In H. Murphy (Ed.), *Proceedings of the Sixth Annual Conference, Technology and Persons with Disabilities* (pp. 815-826), California State University, Northridge.

Scherer, M.J. (1991c). *Psychosocial factors associated with women's use of technological assistance.* Paper presented at the 99th annual convention of the American Psychological Association, San Francisco. (Cassette Recording No. APA-91-306).

Scherer, M.J. (1990). Assistive device utilization and quality of life in adults with spinal cord injuries or cerebral palsy: Two years later. *Journal of Applied Rehabilitation Counseling, 21*(4), 36-44.

Scherer, M.J. (1988). Assistive device utilization and quality of life in adults with spinal cord injuries or cerebral palsy. *Journal of Applied Rehabilitation Counseling, 19*(2), 21-30.

Scherer, M.J. (1988). Differing perspectives of the use of assistive technology devices (ATDs) by people with physical disabilities. In H. Murphy (Ed.), *Proceedings of the Fourth Annual Conference, "Technology and Persons with Disabilities"* (pp. 444-453). Los Angeles: Office of Disabled Student Services, California State University, Northridge.

Scherer, M.J. (1986). Values in the creation, prescription, and use of technological aids and assistive devices for people with physical disabilities. Doctoral dissertation, University of Rochester, and final report to the National Science Foundation. *Dissertation Abstracts International*, 48(01), 49. (University Microfilms No. ADG87-08247).

Scherer, M.J. (1984). A descriptive study of regional spinal cord injured data bases with special emphasis on selected variables in the base managed by Strong Memorial Hospital. Unpublished paper,

University of Rochester School of Medicine and Dentistry, Department of Preventive, Family, and Rehabilitation Medicine.

Scherer, M.J. & McKee, B.G. (1991). *The development of two instruments assessing the predispositions people have toward technology use: The value of integrating quantitative and qualitative methods.* Paper presented at the 1991 annual meeting of the American Educational Research Association, Chicago. (ERIC Document No. TM016608).

Scherer, M.J. & McKee, B.G. (1989). *The Assistive Technology Device Predisposition Assessment (ATD PA)*, Rochester, NY.

Scherer, M.J. McKee, B.G. & Young, M.A. (1990). *The Educational Technology Predisposition Assessment (ET PA).* Rochester, NY.

Scherer, M.J. & Weissberger, R.M. (1989). *The Technology Overload Assessment (TOA).* Rochester, NY.

Schwartz, David B. (1992) *Crossing the River: Creating a Conceptual Revolution in Community and Disability.* Cambridge, MA: Brookline Books.

Schweitzer, JR. (1989). Considerations for procurement of devices and equipment: Shopping for assistive devices. In P. Hale (Ed.), *Rehabilitation Technology Services: A guide for the Rehabilitation Counselor* (pp. 27-29). Baton Rouge: Center for Rehabilitation Science and Biomedical Engineering, Louisiana Tech University.

Siegel, B.S. (1986). *Love, medicine, and miracles.* New York: Harper & Row.

Siegel, B.S. (1989). *Peace, love and healing.* New York: Harper & Row.

Skow, J. (August 17, 1987). Heroism, hugs and laughter. *Time,* 60.

Sontag, S. (1978). *Illness as metaphor.* New York: Farrar, Straus and Giroux.

Sontag, S. (1989). *AIDS and its metaphors.* New York: Farrar, Straus and Giroux.

Starkey. P.D. (1967). Sick role retention as a factor in nonrehabilitation. *Journal of Counseling Psychology, 15*(1), 75-79.

Stoll, K. (1983/1). Laughter is part of a survivor's handbook. *Disabled USA,* 10-12.

Stubbins, J. (Ed.). (1977). *Social and psychological aspects of disability: A handbook for practitioners.* Baltimore: University Park Press.

Summers, M. & Joslyn-Scherer, M. (1982). UCPA puts technology to work. *Advocacy News,* 2(3), 1, 6.

Szalai, A. & Andrews, F.M. (1980). *The quality of life: Comparative studies.* Beverly Hills, CA: Sage Publications, Inc.

Thomason, TC. (1990). Assistive technology for rural American Indians. In H. Murphy (Ed.), *Proceedings of the Fifth Annual Conference, "Technology and Persons with Disabilities"* (pp. 695-701). Los Angeles: Office of Disabled Student Services, California State University, Northridge.

Trieschmann, R.B. (1988). *Spinal cord injuries: Psychological, social, and vocational rehabilitation* (2nd ed.). New York: Demos Publications.

Ulicny, G.R., White, G.W., Bradford, B. & Mathews, R.M. (1990). Consumer exploitation by attendants: How often does it happen and can anything be done about it? *Rehabilitation Counseling Bulletin, 33*(3), 240-246.

U.S. Department of Health, Education, and Welfare. (1978). *The White House conference on handicapped individuals: Summary final report.* (DHEW Publication No. (OHD) 78-22003). Washington, D.C.: Author.

University of Wisconsin, Stout. (October, 1984). *Discovery '84: Technology for disabled persons.* Author.

Vash, C.L. (1981). *The psychology of disability.* New York: Springer Publishing Co.

Vash, C.L. (1983). Psychological aspects of rehabilitation engineering. In *Technology for independent living II*, M. Redden & V. Stern (Eds.). Washington, DC: American Association for the Advancement of Science.

Welch, R.D., Lobley, S.J., O'Sullivan, S.B., & Freed, M.M. (1985). Functional independence in quadriplegia: Critical levels. *Archives of Physical Medicine & Rehabilitation, 67*, 235-240.

Whiteneck, G.G., Charlifue, S.W., Frankel, H.L., Fraser, M.H., Gardner, B.P., Gerhart, K.A., Krishnan, K.R., Menter, R.R., Nuseibeh, I., Short, D.J., & Silver, J.R. (1992). Mortality, morbidity, and psychosocial outcomes of persons spinal cord injured more than 20 years ago. *Paraplegia, 30*, 617-630.

Wright, B.A. (1960). *Physical disability: A psychological approach.* New York: Harper & Row.

Zola, I.K. (1972). Medicine as an institution of social control. *Sociological Review, 20*, 487-504.

Zola, I.K. (1984). Disincentives to independent living. In *Proceedings of the 2nd International Conference on Rehabilitation Engineering* (pp. 121-125), Washington, D.C.: RESNA Press.

Glossary

Adapted Devices/
Equipment: a term used to refer to devices designed for the general population but are adapted in ways to be useful for people with disabilities (for example, eating utensils with built-up handles).

ADL: Activities of Daily Living; those tasks that a person performs during a typical day (grooming, bathing, etc.).

Adventitiously
Disabled: Receiving a disability after the acquisition of language and after early socialization.

Assistive Technology
Device: as defined in the "Technology-Related Assistance of Individuals with Disabilities Act of 1988" (P.L. 100-407): is "any item, piece of equipment, or product system, whether acquired commercially off the shelf, modified, or customized, that is used to increase, maintain, or improve functional capabilities of individuals with disabilities." An assistive device can be low-tech (mechanical) or high-tech (electro-mechanical or computerized) and includes products that compensate for sensory and functional losses by providing the means to move (e.g. wheelchairs, lifts), speak (e.g. voice synthesizers), read (e.g. Opticon systems for persons who are blind), hear (e.g. vibro-tactile aids) and manage self-care tasks (e.g. automatic feeders, environmental control systems).

Service: as defined in the "Technology-Related Assistance of Individuals with Disabilities Act of 1988" (P.L. 100-

407): "any service that directly assists an individual with a disability in the selection, acquisition, or use of an assistive technology device."

Communication Devices

AAC: Augmentative and alternative communication systems: technologies that enable a person with limited speech or no useable speech to visually display their words or speak through synthesized speech output.

word-board: a stiff, flat surface that contains the letters of the alphabet, numbers 1-10, and perhaps many key phrases such as 'thank you,' 'I want,' and so on. It is small and light enough to hold in one's lap. The user of a wordboard communicates by spelling out words.

Congenital Disability:

A disability present before, during or immediately after birth.

Coping:

According To Beatrice Wright, "[Seeing] the difficulties associated with a disability as something that [can] be faced in some way or overcome...[focusing] on the adjustable aspects... coping with the difficulties rather than managing because of blissful ignorance or pretense."

Environmental Control System (ECS):

activates a variety of household appliances such as a coffee maker, TV, radio, lights, automatic dialing telephones, and intercoms through a mouthstick, a puff-and-sip pneumatic control (for those with enough ventilatory control), or through a voice-activated mechanism.

Independent Living:

a philosophy advocating self-directed choice and the ability to exercise as many free choices as possible.

Normalization: a philosophy that people with disabilities can be helped to exhibit personal, social, and work behaviors as close to "normal" as possible and they should be treated no differently from anyone else. Without denying the presence of a disability, proponents of normalization work for the elimination of special treatment and privileges and gave birth to such ideas as educational mainstreaming.

Orthotic Devices: used to provide support for a weak part of the body (e.g. braces).

OVR: Office/Division of Vocational Rehabilitation. A state agency that provides services to help persons with disabilities who are seeking employment.

**Personal
Assistance:**   Care provided by individuals to help persons with disabilities in ADL and other activities. May be provided by family members, paid individuals, etc.

**Prosthetic
Devices:**   replace or substitute a part of the body (like arms and legs)and include artificial limbs.

Rehabilitation: The working definition of "rehabilitation" used by most professionals in the field emphasizes the restoration of a person's physical, sensory, mental, emotional, social, vocational, and recreational capacities so the person can be as autonomous as possible and will be able to pursue an independent non-institutional lifestyle.

Index